Interpreters vs Machines

From tech giants to plucky startups, the world is full of companies boasting that they are on their way to replacing human interpreters, but are they right? *Interpreters vs Machines* offers a solid introduction to recent theory and research on human and machine interpreting, and then invites the reader to explore the future of interpreting. With a foreword by Dr Henry Liu, the 13th International Federation of Translators (FIT) President, and written by consultant interpreter and researcher Jonathan Downie, this book offers a unique combination of research and practical insight into the field of interpreting.

Written in an innovative, accessible style with humorous touches and real-life case studies, this book is structured around the metaphor of playing and winning a computer game. It takes interpreters of all experience levels on a journey to better understand their own work, learn how computers attempt to interpret and explore possible futures for human interpreters.

With five levels and split into 14 chapters, *Interpreters vs Machines* is key reading for all professional interpreters as well as students and researchers of Interpreting and Translation Studies, and those with an interest in machine interpreting.

Jonathan Downie is a consultant interpreter, French to English and English to French conference and business interpreter, researcher and speaker on interpreting. He regularly writes on the connections between research in practice in interpreting and translation for the *ITI Bulletin* and *VKD Kurier*. He is the author of the award-winning and critically acclaimed *Being a Successful Interpreter: Adding Value and Delivering Excellence.*

Interpreters vs Machines

Can Interpreters Survive in an AI-Dominated World?

Jonathan Downie

Routledge
Taylor & Francis Group

LONDON AND NEW YORK

First published 2020
by Routledge
2 Park Square, Milton Park, Abingdon, Oxon OX14 4RN

and by Routledge
52 Vanderbilt Avenue, New York, NY 10017

Routledge is an imprint of the Taylor & Francis Group, an informa business

© 2020 Jonathan Downie

British Library Cataloguing-in-Publication Data
A catalogue record for this book is available from the British Library

Library of Congress Cataloging-in-Publication Data
Names: Downie, Jonathan, author.
Title: Interpreters vs machines: can interpreters survive in an
AI-dominated world? / Jonathan Downie.
Description: London; New York, NY: Routledge, 2020. |
Includes bibliographical references and index.
Identifiers: LCCN 2019038124 | ISBN 9781138586420 (hardback) |
ISBN 9781138586437 (paperback) | ISBN 9781003001805 (ebook)
Subjects: LCSH: Translating and interpreting. | Machine translating.
Classification: LCC P306 .D69 2020 | DDC 418/.020285–dc23
LC record available at https://lccn.loc.gov/2019038124

ISBN: 978-1-138-58642-0 (hbk)
ISBN: 978-1-138-58643-7 (pbk)
ISBN: 978-1-003-00180-5 (ebk)

Typeset in Times New Roman and Gill Sans
by Deanta Global Publishing Services, Chennai, India

Visit the eResources: www.routledge.com/9781138586437

Contents

Foreword

Predicting the future may be a fool's game; preparing for the future certainly is not.

Such preparation took many forms, building ramparts, digging moats, spreading disinformation and even silencing opposition – just to name a few.

Not surprisingly, the reputed second oldest profession and the wider language service industry worth US$46.52 billion[1] are no different.

There are the establishment steadfastly defending the status quo, rebels blowing up the foundations and the so-called disrupters whose only achievement remains disrupting other people's salary and security. And then there are the bewildered interpreting students. Meanwhile, the public is totally ambivalent.

Unlike the hype of autonomous vehicles, which are often featured in my keynote addresses, most people on the streets of Manchester, Moscow or Mumbai will have little interest in Machine Translation and even less for machine interpreting, let alone any knowledge of the wider social implication thereof.

Following on from the success of his first book and the cult-status podcasts by the Troublesome Terps Troika, Dr Jonathan Downie has penned a witty guide to this seemingly fool's game in this totally unique and dystopically titled volume.

Whom do you trust?

The trinitarian axioms of interpreting – accuracy, impartiality, confidentiality – which brought about the boom in interpreting from conference to community in the second half of the 20th century as well as the current status of our profession, were a modern construct which arose, to a large degree, from the power asymmetry and multilateralism in the atmosphere of distrust of foreignness.

So what is the modern currency of trust?

Who interprets matters

Fighting against machine interpreting on the grounds of beauty or ethics or even human rights is a sure-fire way to be on the losing side.

(This volume, p. 6)

Does this mean ethics or aesthetics do not matter in the AI-dominated world?

The paradox of AI is that on the one hand, it purportedly promises large-scale, high-speed reproducibility whilst its inner workings are obscured from view or scrutiny. Would politicians or business leaders trust tech to convey their intention and implement their strategy? How about the less powerful? Should we allow asylum seekers' fate to be determined by machines, which is happening at a border somewhere right now?

Where have all the interpreters gone?

I have previously argued in Help or Hinder[2] that technology has increasingly obscured the interpreters from the sight of and therefore connection with those who depends on us.

As this volume goes to print, there are over two million views of the Wired Masterminds' "Interpreter Breaks Down How Real-Time Translation Works," featuring Barry Olsen.

It is such positive visibility, career prospects and status which translate into enrolment in T&I schools, thereby disrupting a dangerous self-fulling prophecy that threatens our very future.

Allons Enfants de la Patrie

Where do we begin? I am confident you will find insights and answers in Downie's latest volume, from refocusing on "softer" and core skills, becoming mindful of the PR consequences of our actions, to actively engaging with your professional association.

We know we cannot do it alone, as individual interpreters. So let's make sure that no colleague will ever say "whatever I get paid to do" at the next dinner party. Only then can we not only survive but thrive in an AI-dominated world.

Henry Liu
13th FIT President
Auckland, New Zealand

Notes

1   2018 Common Sense Advisory.
2   http://www3.uah.es/fitispos_ij/OJS/ojs-2.4.5/index.php/fitispos/article/view/162.

Acknowledgements

As much as a book might have a single author on the front cover, all books are all the result of an unbelievable amount of team effort. I would therefore like to thank:

- My wife, Helen, for believing in me enough to encourage me to write my first book and then supporting me through the second. There is absolutely no way that either book would exist without her love and sacrifice,
- The team at Routledge, who nurtured both books, spotted my errors, added flair to my style, cut my waffle and did their best to make both books a success,
- The dynamic duo that is Alexander Drechsel and Alexander Gansmeier. Doing Troublesome Terps together is a dream and has become a real fountain of ideas. Our two episodes on machine interpreting helped to refine my thinking and showed me that this book was definitely a good idea,
- Every single person whom I have interviewed, probed and queried for this book, including: Prof Andy Way, Tommi Niemanen, Alistair Turner, Prof Kilian Seeber, Ewandro Magalhaes, Prof Barry Olsen, Dr Henry Liu and many, many more,
- The late and very great, Esther Navarro-Hall, whose presence in the interpreting community is sorely missed and whose influence I hope will be felt for a long time,
- Judy and Dagmar Jenner, whose book still inspires me and who never fail to be an encouragement to interpreters everywhere,
- Sarah Bawa Mason, not only for being an incredible chair of ITI but for the opportunity to get involved in writing open letters, and for her support when I presented early thinking from this book at the APTRAD conference in Portugal,
- The team at APTRAD for inviting me to speak at that conference,
- The ITI conference team for inviting me to speak in Sheffield,
- Elaine Simpson and the National Library of Scotland team for managing to find the books and resources I needed while I wrote,

- My friends and church family at City Gates Baptist Church for all of your incredible support over the years,
- Prof Graham Turner, whose support and partnership in research made this book possible,
- And my four amazing children: Joshua, Hope, Gemma and Emily, for putting up with Daddy disappearing off to the National Library of Scotland one day a week to get the book finished. It's finished now.

Introduction

Excellent interpreting is priceless. It is the difference between successful negotiations and diplomatic incidents, between a recovering patient and a medical malpractice charge, between a Deaf child learning and yet another case of social and economic isolation. It changes the lives of those who experience it and determines the course of history.

Yet interpreting is under threat like never before. When I wrote *Being a Successful Interpreter: Adding Value and Delivering Excellence*, there were rumbles of a coming crisis. Now, with technology giants like Google and Tencent applying their seemingly unlimited resources to machine interpreting and platform after platform being launched to leverage economies of scale and big data to squeeze prices, the need to secure the future of our profession has never been more pressing.

But what should we do? What does the future of interpreting look like, faced with the might of the biggest technology companies on the planet? Is it time for interpreters to retreat to the big international institutions, demand legal protection and prepare to be phased out?

No responsible commentator could do anything but treat seriously the possibility that one day human interpreters may be eliminated or sentenced to work entirely remotely, chained to their desks. Yet no serious interpreter would be satisfied with either of those futures. The rest of this book will deliberately and systematically examine several possibilities for the future of interpreting and present strategies to ensure that the future of interpreting is skilled, rewarding and most of all, human.

Before that, however, there are foundations that need to be laid and stories that need to be told. No one would ever accept a vaccination without being convinced of the seriousness of the disease it prevents. No interpreters should even consider making significant shifts in their working methods, marketing and PR until they understand where the profession is now, how it got here and the pros and cons of any changes they might make.

That's why this book starts with an outline of some fundamental concepts and understandings of what interpreting is and how it works. Those used to playing computer games can treat these as the gameplay guide. Yes, you can try to mash the controls and skip through levels, but that route leads to frustration and slow progress. If we are going to learn how to survive and thrive in an AI-dominated world, we need to know our strengths and the strengths of the algorithms we face, the shape of the levels and most of all, the destination we want to reach.

Like a good computer game, this book is arranged in levels, building up from material on the very basics of what interpreting is and how it is done all the way up to a step-by-step plan to keep humans at the forefront of interpreting.

Level 1 covers the fundamentals. Its three chapters cover topics that every interpreter should know but few will have time to study. Chapter 1 poses the simple but profound question "What is interpreting?" With research continuing to question the accuracy of many of the views of interpreting held by established professionals and with machines getting closer to delivering something that could be deemed accuracy, the way we answer this single question will have a profound impact on our future.

There are two main views of interpreting that we need to grapple with: the traditional conduit model and the newer triadic model. Both models are explained in detail and their pros and cons are discussed. I will also give some practical examples of what conduit interpreting and triadic interpreting would look like in interpreting assignments.

Chapter 2 asks the more technical question "How do humans interpret?" If you ask credible interpreting researchers, they will most likely reply that we actually don't know how humans interpret. There are models, theories and experiments covering different parts of the interpreting process, but even these have been challenged by the realisation that, outside of the laboratory, interpreting is an interpersonal skill.

For that reason, Chapter 2 won't offer a simple, perfect answer to the question but will instead fuse together research on interpreter cognition with research on interpreter decision making to offer an account of the factors that go into expert interpreting performance.

Chapter 3 turns the spotlight on the bots and asks how computers "interpret." The quotation marks are used deliberately. The truth is that with the advent of machine learning, neural networks, big data and numerous other technological buzzword-laden discoveries, computers can do new and surprising things with data. But that is all it ever is: data. This chapter will provide a brief, non-technical overview of the big technological advances in modern machine interpreting, exploring their strengths and exposing their weaknesses. Given the speed at which progress is made, the summary will stay at a fairly general level, with some very specific examples given. It will also cover in brief why it is a mistake to label any of the technologies and algorithms used in machine interpreting as "AI," despite the title of this book.

Understanding the fundamentals of what interpreting is and how humans and computers (attempt to) do it, provides the background for **Level 2**, which examines how interpreting got to its current position of being established as a profession but now losing ground to the big technology companies pushing machine interpreting.

Chapter 4 delves into the world of interpreter Public Relations (PR) and asks how interpreters have presented themselves and their work to potential clients and to the world at large. Based on some excellent sleuthing by researchers such as Ebru Diriker, as well as real-life experience, this chapter provides an honest account of how, in their attempts to present themselves as arch-professionals, interpreters have often accidentally presented their work in such a way as to make it look like computers could take over.

The counterpoint to limited interpreter PR is the wild and nearly unbelievable claims made by providers of machine interpreting, which are examined in Chapter 5. Based on actual advertising and promotional materials for machine interpreting devices and apps, this chapter plots the main claims and benefits promoted by the machine interpreting industry and, with two doses of cheek, gets to the bottom of what these companies are actually selling to consumers.

Faulty interpreting PR and slick PR to promote machine interpreting have meant that even many professional interpreters might fear for their future. Rather than present a long, involved argument for what interpreting might look like in the future, this book lets you make that choice. In **Level 3**: "Choose Your Interpreting Future," you are in control, deciding what the future of interpreting will look like and discovering the consequences that come with each choice.

You can choose from a future where human interpreting is nothing more than a stopgap until machines get good enough to replace them (Chapter 6), human interpreters keeping their jobs due to robust legal protection (Chapter 7), humans being limited to a small number of niches (Chapter 8) or a new future for interpreting, where human interpreting is the gold standard (Chapter 9).

If human interpreting is to become the universally recognised gold standard, then interpreters will need to make changes to the way they promote, market and deliver their work, which is the subject of **Level 4**. Given the historical weakness of interpreter PR, taking back control of how the world sees interpreting will be the first step and is the topic of Chapter 10. At this level, interpreters will need to learn how to tell stories about the value of their work, speak in relevant ways about wider societal issues and demonstrate how almost every sector of the economy, every cause and every business deal is touched by interpreting.

Solid PR provides the foundation for marketing interpreting, and Chapter 11 provides an outline of what it means to market interpreting effectively to clients. If PR makes the public more aware of what interpreting can do, marketing makes individual companies and organisations aware of what interpreting can do for them. The stories that gained public interest and improved PR need to be turned into case studies that lead potential clients towards bringing in human interpreters for their most important deals. This chapter provides some hands-on case studies for how this works in practice.

Chapter 12 deals with the kind of interpreting delivered to clients. While accuracy will always be the core of interpreting, this chapter argues for interpreters to understand what is needed in each situation for their interpreting to make a positive contribution to the events at which they work. This chapter will therefore examine the key features of interpreting that delivers more than words.

Consistently delivering high-value interpreting requires more than language skills and good technique. Chapter 13 calls for all interpreters to take part in mentoring or coaching relationships to ensure that their skills are always improving, no matter their career stage.

Like all good computer games, the final level comes with a surprise. In this case, **Level 5** asks whether our determination to fight for the future of human interpreting might miss the best possible solution of all.

The most important idea to keep in mind while reading this book is that no matter what we read in the press or on social media, the future of interpreting is in the hands of interpreters. The rest of this book is there to help you deal with that reality.

Level I

The fundamentals

I still remember it now, even though I must have been only about five or six years old when we got it. Family legend says that my dad saved up for months to buy it and, on the Christmas Eve when he set it up with one of his mates and a couple of my uncles, they missed the Watchnight service at church because they were busy "testing" it until 3:00 a.m.

Eventually, it got moved to the bedroom I shared with my older brother. My children are confused by how much simpler it was then. Its capabilities are laughably limited compared to anything you could buy for the same amount of money now. But at the time, the thought never occurred to me that within a few short years, it would be obsolete and within a decade or so, it would be all but forgotten, its stark green lines and tiny frame dwarfed by the white aluminium casing of our newer model.

You never forget the first computer you use. Ours was an *Amstrad CPC 464*. It couldn't do much but it did enough to keep us busy and entertained for years.

Could it be that computers might soon be so capable that they make the final leap from green-screened noisy boxes with limited memory and clunky keys to becoming fully capable of replacing humans?

No single book can answer that question for all possible futures. Even answering the interpreting version of that question takes hard work and careful thinking. For a start, interpreting itself is a startlingly complicated profession. From sign language interpreting in universities to spoken language interpreting in hospices, there are no facets of human life that interpreting doesn't touch in some way. Before we start predicting the future of interpreting, we need to know what interpreting is and what exactly the inventors of machine interpreting are trying to do.

Since technology is the theme of this book, it helps to break down the journey towards the future of interpreting as if you were going through different levels of a computer game. As I mentioned in the introduction, this level is where we learn the basics: what the aim of the game is, what the basic controls are, where the "game" might be taking us.

That's what this section is about. As tempting as it might be to throw away the manual and wade into the game, hoping that you can learn on the go, that route leads to nothing but dead ends and frustration. Instead, let's begin by answering the apparently simple and fundamental but actually fiendishly complex questions that are at the heart of any prediction of the future of interpreting: what is interpreting?, how do humans interpret? and how do computers try to interpret?

Chapter 1

What is interpreting?

So what is interpreting? What seems like a simple question is actually the source of controversy, confusion and misunderstanding. Are we dictionaries on legs, filled with excellent terminology but hardly a human emotion? Are we conduits, who just say what the original speaker said, no more, no less? Are we mediators, who find the middle ground between two opposing interests? Are we activists who use our considerable power to make the world a better place?

What actually is an interpreter? Rather than giving a philosophical answer, I think it makes more sense to start with a story.

The interpreter believes that there has been a misunderstanding

Every interpreter has a favourite interpreting story. This is mine:

> It was a bracingly cold day somewhere in central Scotland. I had been asked by one of my agency clients to interpret at a "sales qualification meeting." It sounds fancier than it was. Basically, a buyer had flown in from France to go through a questionnaire on company policies, finances and product quality with representatives of a British company. Their answers to the questionnaire and his impression from a tour of their facilities would decide whether they got a multi-year, multi-million-pound contract.

> I didn't know all of that. I knew the British company well and I had studied its target client. I had studied the French questionnaire and knew what was likely to come up. I didn't know how big the deal was likely to be (the British company didn't even know that!) and, most importantly, I didn't know that the company had translated the questionnaire in-house and answered "as best as they could" with their "in-house French knowledge."

> That last little piece of information would prove to be more important than anyone could have imagined.

The tour went well. I got some free education from the Brits, who were very keen to show off their expertise on how to make those specific products, and from the French buyer, who was keen to show that he had once run a facility just like the one they were seeing. The rest of the first day was fairly standard stuff: the usual yawn-inducing presentation of the British company and its client book, some semi-technical presentations and some pretty standard chat about dashboards and KPIs.

Midway through the second day, the atmosphere changed dramatically. It started with an offhand remark from the French buyer. He wondered aloud why the British company was scoring very poorly for quality on its question-naire when the tour had reassured him that it was actually producing excellent products.

And then it all kicked off. Within less than half an hour, what had been a con-genial meeting turned into a stand-off. The French buyer felt that the British company was being deliberately evasive. The British company felt that the French buyer was asking the same questions again and again when they had already answered them. Chairs were pulled back from the table. First the British technical director, then the French buyer and then everyone else stood up and made for the door. We marched along corridors through sets of heavy double doors. Fingers poked charts on the walls. Heads shook. I am sure I heard a few exasperated sighs.

In one wondrous moment, I had a realisation:

"The interpreter believes there has been a misunderstanding."

Those weren't the exact words I used, but they are close enough. In under a minute, I explained what had suddenly become obvious to me. The French client wanted to know the proportion of pieces that the British company was producing with *no* defects. The British company was used to measuring the number they produced *with* defects.

The relief was almost as tangible as the lunchtime sandwiches had been. A very relieved technical director smiled "Och, is that all he wants? C'mere and I'll get those stats for you."

Less than five minutes later, a happy French buyer was casting his eyes over a spreadsheet with the exact numbers he wanted. Within about two hours, happy handshakes matched jolly smiles, the British company was in receipt of permission to request a test order and, so long as the products were as good as they were said to be, a very nice multi-year contract was on its way to being signed. It would be a nice bonus when the chief executive of the British company would end the day assuring me that, even though he spoke French, they could not have done the deal without me.

Unpacking the story

Depending on the kind of interpreting you do, that story might seem fairly typical. In many cases, the success of an event, business deal or medical appointment hinges on the interpreter's expertise and decision-making. In those environments, tiny decisions make a big difference. Do you explain a term or keep it as is? What do you do with that joke? What do you do if the parties misunderstand each other?

Good interpreting is the ability to take such decisions intelligently. The truth is that even if we want to keep using the traditional definition of interpreters as being impartial, accurate and terminologically exact, there will always be decisions we take as to how to solve specific problems. Those decisions are rarely clear-cut.

Stories like the one I just told show that there is a lot more going on than simply fetching the French equivalent of a word in English or the correct Hindi expression for a German phrase. Language comes with baggage, and it is always dangerous to assume that an accurate rendition of what was said will leave no room for misunderstanding and ambiguity. On the contrary, the very fact that language is tied inseparably to culture means that no term or phrase can ever be isolated from the culture in which it originated, no matter how much dictionaries and term bases might try to tell us otherwise.

Interpreters jump headlong into this potential confusion and have to try to find a way to swim to the other side of it. While lexicographers, terminologists and etymologists might bask in words for the sake of words, interpreters have to be aware that words are always doing something: expressing emotion or attitude, creating new realities, explaining, informing, goading, playing, deceiving, even flirting. For interpreting to work, words or signs must be found that do the same things in an appropriate way in an entirely different language.

Even the account I've just provided of interpreting is not enough. Interpreters don't just play with words and reflect on the possibility of mutual understanding. No client ever hires interpreters because they want some theoretical account of terminological equivalence between Dutch and Swahili. For clients, interpreting isn't important because of what it *is* but because of what it *does*. It might sound mercenary, but clients always want interpreting for their own reasons. They have treatment to administer, deals to strike, staff to hire or sack, treaties to sign, possible suppliers or customers to wow, journalists to tame or blame, details to explain or some other thing to do or achieve.

To interpret is to help someone achieve something that they could not otherwise achieve. Interpreting is purposeful, and its purpose may be only tangentially related to language.

The story I just told is a simple example of that premise. The purpose of the *meeting* was not to have accurate interpreting but to sell products. The purpose of the *interpreting* was to enable products to be sold. The *need* for interpreting only arose because the client happened to be French. The *act* and *accuracy* of interpreting were only important because of what they allowed the client to do. If that seems to go against our rarefied view of our job, then it may be because many of us love interpreting so much that it hurts to realise that, for our clients, it is merely a means to an end. And a rather expensive means at that.

Before we do any work towards defending human interpreting against the big bad boss of machine interpreting, we need to swallow that healthy dose of reality. Fighting against machine interpreting on the grounds of beauty or ethics or even human rights is a sure-fire way to be on the losing side. Building a case for human interpreting on the basis of its unique contribution to business growth or fair legal proceedings or more effective medical care or any of the hundreds of other tangible reasons for our work will be much more effective. Put simply, it's not enough to prove to clients that they *need* interpreting; they need to be convinced that they actually *want* it.

It's not enough to prove to clients that they *need* interpreting; they need to be convinced that they actually *want* it.

The first stage in building that kind of case is to have a realistic model of interpreting in terms of our relationship with the people for whom we interpret. To get to that point, we first need to understand two basic models of interpreting. Both are simplified representations of what interpreters do, but both have a lot to tell us about the nature of our work.

Enter the conduit model

Until the mid-1990s, there was only one model of interpreting in town, and it was a view that was held nearly universally, by interpreters and clients alike. In this model, the interpreter was nothing more or less than a communication channel through which people spoke when they needed their words to be understood by someone who didn't speak the same language.

In a manner similar to landline telephones, interpreters were basically seen as taking a signal in one language, turning it into an exact representation in another language and passing it on. The best interpreting was therefore interpreting where there was no loss or gain in this process. The premise was simple: just say exactly what was said in the other language.

The name "conduit model" was borrowed from researchers looking at how people thought about communication processes in general (notably Reddy, 1979) but would prove to be a useful term. After all, in this view of interpreting, the interpreter had little more intrinsic value than a pipe or an electric cable.

To fully understand this model of interpreting, it helps to have a diagram. The most famous diagram to describe the conduit model is found in the work of Shannon (1948). His model was about communication in general. Figure 1.1 is a simpler, more interpreting-specific version inspired by his work.

Figure 1.1 The conduit model of interpreting.

In the conduit model, communication begins with the source language speaker, who wants to share some piece of information but cannot because they don't speak the same language as the audience. In between the speaker and the audience, therefore, stands the interpreter, whose role it is to stand between them and make communication possible.

In this model, the principal point at which something can go wrong is with the interpreter. It is here and only here that there is the possibility of interpreting breaking down. It could be something as simple as poor ambient conditions or something as complex as poor preparation or the interpreter being biased. What matters is that, in the conduit model, if it all goes wrong, it is interpreter's fault. As the bridge between the speaker and audience and the sole route by which communication can flow, the interpreter is both the key point of communication and its single point of failure.

Yes, it is possible that there is some issue between the source language speaker thinking of an idea and expressing it, but in the conduit model such a possibility is rarely discussed. There could equally be a problem with the target language audience misunderstanding something, but again, that is not something most accounts of this model deal with. In fact, even when such possibilities are discussed, conduit-model thinking excludes any possibility of the interpreter taking action to resolve the issue. In the video "Spoken and written in conference interpreting, Part 2,"[1] translation scholar Anthony Pym points out that some issues with Spanish court interpreting in parts of the USA have been traced to the low educational attainment level of some of the immigrants appearing before the courts. His suggestion that, in the interests of a fair trial, interpreters might want to adjust their language register to make up for the deficit was met with horror by the interpreting students at the lecture.

The logic is simple: in court, the interpreter is not supposed to add or omit anything. Changing register must be some kind of addition or omission; therefore, it is impossible to even consider.

Whether you agree with that view or not, it is classic conduit-model thinking. The role of the interpreter is to simply say what was said. If any problems arise because of what was said or how it was said, that is for everyone else to deal with. In the conduit model, we are "just there to interpret" and interpreting is limited to what was said by the source language speaker.

The conduit model is designed to be an expressly limiting model of interpreting. It presents interpreters with black-and-white options that aim to keep them in the role of simply relaying what was said and to limit the responsibility of the interpreter to producing accurate renditions.

The influence of the conduit model is everywhere. For all its emphasis on interpreters thinking actively and being professionals, the much vaunted "Theory of Sense" or Paris School of interpreting (read, for example, Seleskovitch, 1968; Seleskovitch and Lederer, 1984) is basically the conduit model with improved knowledge of linguistics. At its core is the idea that interpreters hear what is said, "deverbalise" it and then turn that "deverbalised" version into a representation in the target language. This idea will be come back in the next chapter, but what is important to realise about this model of interpreting is that it essentially still sees interpreting as something done between two different *languages*, rather than between two or more *people*. Even though the point of the Theory of Sense is that interpreters need to discover the meaning of what was said and will therefore inevitably rely on some contextual knowledge, this contextual knowledge is mostly about the co-text of the speech (read, for example, Seleskovitch, 1975) rather than the fact that Mr Jones is famous for making culturally unacceptable jokes or that Herr Schmidt is desperately trying to convince some Brazilian clients to buy some shoes from him.

The conduit-model definition of interpreting

Ask an adherent of the conduit model to define interpreting and you will be likely to get a response that emphasises the role of the interpreter as someone who passes on what was said whilst remaining completely impartial. In fact, they may even go so far as to claim that interpreters should be so good that it's as if they weren't even there. A good test of whether someone is a fan of the conduit model is to give them this situation from the work of conference interpreter trainer and interpreting researcher Andrew Clifford and ask them to tell you how the interpreter should respond.

> Imagine that you are an experienced community interpreter, working primarily in the field of healthcare. You are asked to interpret a medical appointment, and you have worked with both the physician and the patient before. The physician runs a busy family practice. He works on a fee-for-service model, and he pays hefty overhead and insurance. He is under intense pressure to move patients through his office quickly, in order to cover his costs. To further complicate matters, the physician sees a large number of patients who are HIV positive, and who have complex medical needs. Most times, these patients require more time from the physician than he can realistically give. He works long hours and weekends to keep up with the demand.
>
> The patient is a relative newcomer to Canada. She moved here just under a year ago with her husband and her children. Like many women in her cultural community, she stayed at home to look after her children, and she has had little contact with broader Canadian society. She speaks almost no English. Her husband worked outside the home and took responsibility for

communication with the community at large. Unfortunately, six months after arriving in Canada, the patient's husband became seriously ill (he told his wife he had "leukaemia"), and he passed away three weeks prior to the medical appointment you are interpreting. The patient was understandably devastated. A short time after her husband's death, the patient had a meeting with another healthcare practitioner – the details are unclear – but the patient was told "horrible things" about her husband that she could not believe. That her husband had been having sex with men. That he had not died of leukaemia but of AIDS. During the meeting, a blood sample was taken, and an appointment was made for the patient to see the busy family doctor. She arrives for the appointment struggling to understand all that has happened to her. She is bewildered and afraid.

You are sitting in an examination room with the patient when the physician enters suddenly and brusquely. He sits down at his desk and shuffles some papers. He picks up a printout, turns to the patient, and says, "Yup, you're positive."

Both the physician and the patient turn to you for the interpretation. What do you do?

(Clifford, 2004, p. 89)

The classic conduit model response is that the interpreter should ignore the background context and simply say the target language version of "Yep, you're positive." In the conduit model, that's the extent of the interpreter's role: say what the person said. There may be some quibbling over whether the interpreter should use words that make it clear that the doctor is meaning HIV+, rather than having a positive attitude or being sure of something, but that is extent of the discussion. The classic model says to disregard the effect on the patient or the effect that delivering that information in such a direct way could have on the success of future treatment: just say what needs to be said and move on to the next stretch of speech.

To adherents of the conduit model, interpreting is entirely a linguistic task. Every ethical, technical and strategic decision gets filtered through that definition. Every justification, self-presentation and explanation is founded on that same fundamental ideal. Be the conduit. Be flawless and invisible. Get out of the way and don't worry about the consequences.

This explains why we cannot go any further in discussing strategies to thrive in an AI-dominated world until we grasp our own definitions of interpreting and how they affect our work. To a conduit-model interpreter, the world is full of black-and-white decisions, and every one of these decisions must lead to interpreting being less visible, having less of an impact, making fewer changes.

While it will take later chapters to understand the effects of this kind of thinking on how we present the importance of our work to the public and to potential clients, for now it will suffice to understand that defining interpreting in conduit-model terms reduces both the responsibility of the interpreter and the assumed importance of interpreting itself. It is ironic that lovers of the conduit model want interpreting to be prestigious and respected while arguing that interpreters should be so good that clients can almost ignore their presence. How else can we understand this now famous quote from the AIIC *Practical Guide for Professional Conference Interpreters*?

> [M]ake them [the audience] forget they are hearing the speaker through the interpreter.
>
> (AIIC, 1999, sec. 3.3)

If you like the conduit model, this sounds like the ultimate in perfect interpreting – interpreting so good that it is as if the speaker suddenly learned another language. And indeed, it does sound wonderful – as long as the interpreter is fine with the original speaker getting all the praise and with the client thinking that it doesn't matter much which interpreter they hire, since they are all interchangeable.

At this point, and despite its flaws, it is important to understand the benefits of the conduit model. No one would seriously argue for interpreters to show up and steal the show. The spotlight should be on the speaker and not the interpreter. The patient needs treatment and advice much more than the interpreter needs an ego trip. On that point, the conduit model is a helpful. Interpreters looking to level up their skills could do a lot worse than realising that they are there to serve the other people in the interpreted event.

It is also true that the simplified thinking inherent in the conduit model does create some welcome space to remind interpreters that there should be limits to their role and ethics in their actions. No professional interpreter should think that turning to a patient and saying "Yep, you have AIDS because your husband was a lying philanderer" is a good decision. There must be some ethical limits to our work, especially in sensitive situations.

Yet despite these positives, the conduit model has long been out of favour with researchers, and many training institutions are now teaching an alternative model. Why would that be?

There are three main weaknesses in the conduit model and especially in its definition of interpreting. The first is that, since the mid-1990s, when field research started to unseat experimental research as the principal way of discovering more about interpreting, it has become apparent that there are few, if any, traces of interpreters adhering slavishly to the conduit model in practice. As we will see in the next chapter, interpreters add explanations, summarise, request more information, act as gatekeepers, filter content and more besides, all in the interest of making the meeting a success (see, for example, Wadensjö, 1998; Roy, 1999; Napier, 2004; Beaton, 2007, to name but a few). If the conduit model is the ideal, there is little evidence that any interpreters are even getting close to it.

The second problem is ethical. As Robyn Dean and Robert Pollard (2006) and Dean (2014) have pointed out and as we saw earlier, the conduit model teaches interpreters not to think about the context or consequences of their decisions. Interpreter ethics therefore becomes a set of rules and regulations, rather than a process in which interpreters think intelligently about what is going on and their place in it. It's almost as if they are supposed to be the very machines we are frightened will replace us. Since it tries to distance interpreters from their own humanity and from the humanity of those we work for, the conduit model is the end of good interpreter ethics, not the foundation for it.

> The conduit model is the end of good interpreter ethics, not the foundation for it.

That brings us to the third, and in the context of this book, the most important problem with the conduit model. If the conduit model is correct and interpreting is purely and simply impartial language processing, there is no inherent need for humans to be doing it at all. If accuracy is all there is to interpreting, and computers can be accurate, why should they not take over? This issue forms the backbone of the problem of interpreting PR, covered in Chapters 4 and 11. But for now, it is important to realise that the conduit model cannot provide any convincing arguments for interpreting being carried out by humans rather than machines.

If you read *Being a Successful Interpreter*, you will be familiar with this argument. In this present book, however, I want to show exactly where this argument leads us, especially now that computers are making real improvements in the accuracy and intelligibility of their work. If the conduit model provided the case for clients to reduce interpreter fees and think about replacing us with machines, technological improvements have provided convincing arguments for clients to begin to think seriously about replacing us soon. So where do we find the tools to fight back?

Since those tools cannot be found in the conduit model, we need to look elsewhere. It's time to level up and think about interpreters not as conduits but as members of a team.

Enter the triadic model

I was chuffed. I had just interpreted for a senior Scottish parliamentarian who was speaking to some experts on social policy. It had gone superbly. One of the best shifts of my career so far. I turned off the mic to hand over the shift to my boothmate. A couple of minutes of rest and then I would be ready to help out with any tricky terminology, but given the speaker and the presentation, we didn't expect anything out of the ordinary.

We were wrong. With a beautifully clear Irish accent, the speaker started to go off-script with the immortal and unwelcome line: "Well, since I am in Scotland, I thought I would begin my speech with a quote from Robert

Burns." I have no words to describe the way we felt in the booth right then! But I did seriously consider taking a sly toilet break.

That rather inauspicious start signalled what was to be a real monster of a speech. My boothmate pulled out all the stops and did as well as anyone reasonably could, making sure that both the content and the feeling of the speaker's rather fiery performance were kept in the French rendition. At one particular point, she made what I thought was a brilliant decision. The speaker labelled the British government's treatment of citizens of other EU countries "dis-gus-ting" with a strong emphasis on the "gus" and a face that looked like she had just eaten a particularly sharp lemon. My boothmate did exactly the right thing, finding the French term "dégueulasse," which, as any dictionary will tell you, is right on point.

A member of the French delegation didn't think so. At tea break, he pulled my boothmate aside and told her off for using such a term, even though he had heard and understood the English. "On dirait plutôt « scandaleux »" [we would rather say "scandaleux"], he said.

Hold on a minute! There is no way that any dictionary would equate "dis-gus-ting" with an accent on the "gus" with "scandaleux." "Scandaleux" means "scandalous" or "shocking" or "outrageous." Except right here, right now, for this client, it didn't. It meant "dis-gus-ting," with an emphasis on the "gus." And that was that.

Such stories are common in interpreting and illustrate why the conduit model falls short of describing what actually happens when someone interprets. At the heart of the conduit model is the assumption that meaning is stable and defined outside of any situation. The interpreter hears or sees something, relates it perfectly to a predefined deverbalised equivalent in another language and delivers that equivalent. The problem is precisely that language and interpreting are never that simple. The meaning of a term or phrase or sentence is negotiated in a given context. Clarifications and explanations are often necessary.

As much as interpreting makes possible the hitherto impossible, it always adds a layer of complexity. Adding an interpreter into a situation adds another voice and another speaker. Whether we like it or not, when an interpreter interprets, they become another participant in the event. Their decisions make a difference. Their voice is heard.

This is why we need a new model, the "triadic model," and the power and complexity of interpreting explain why that model is so powerful. In the conduit model, the interpreter is simply a piece of equipment – a channel for communication between the speaker and audience. The less of an impact they make, the better an interpreter we think they are. In the triadic model, we accept right from the start that the interpreter is as much a part of the event as the speaker and audience. Once again, a diagram might help clarify things a bit (see Figure 1.2).

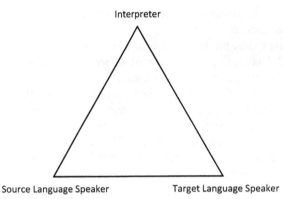

Interpreter

Source Language Speaker   Target Language Speaker

Figure 1.2 The triadic model of interpreting.

The most important thing to notice about the triadic model is that it is based on the idea of interpreting being a team sport. The fundamental view of interpreting in this model is that everyone works together to build understanding (a detailed explanation can be found in Turner (2005)). Everyone has an equal-sized corner of the triangle. In this view, getting the interpreting right is everyone's responsibility. Communication failures can happen at any point.

This leads to the idea that everyone is an equal participant. Yes, the interpreter has a specific role but that specific role is placed alongside that of the speakers (or signers) of the two languages. Once again, we need to remind ourselves that this does not mean that the interpreter steals the show. It does mean, however, that "interpreters are part of the show" (Torres Díaz and Ghignoli, 2014). Exactly what that means and looks like is something that we will examine throughout this book.

There is one more thing worth noting. In the triadic model, unlike the conduit model, there is an assumption that the source language speaker(s) and target language speaker(s) are communicating in some way, even without the interpreter. Most interpreters will recognise times when clients show that they have understood something before we even say it. Just how useful and how accurate that understanding is will vary widely between assignments and between people.

How would adherents of the triadic model define interpreting? For them, interpreting would be the act of working with people who use different languages to help them build mutual understanding.

Yes, there is still a lot wrong with this definition. For a start, it sounds rather fuzzy and non-specific. Mutual understanding of what? What does it mean to work "with" clients? Don't clients all just want interpreters to come in, do their thing invisibly and then go home?

There is also the big question of why mutual understanding is of any interest to clients. Didn't we just say earlier that clients book interpreters so that they can sell shoes, or sign treaties or other things like that? The answer to both questions will be revealed as this book goes on.

Of course, the conduit and triadic models are not the only models of interpreting to have been suggested. Yet most of the other models are closely related to either the conduit model or the triadic model in some way.

We have already touched on how the "Theory of Sense" is more or less aligned with the conduit model. In Sign Language interpreting, there is an older model, the "helper model," in which the interpreter was seen to be helping out the poor Deaf person in need (Wilcox and Shaffer, 2005, p. 29). This model is basically a version of the triadic model gone wrong, with the interpreting being given too much of a position and the Deaf person being subject to the view that they cannot take care of themselves. Something similar happens in professional discussions when interpreters are discussed as being bicultural-bilingual specialists. Once again, in an admirable effort to learn from the triadic model, the status of the interpreter is pumped up, potentially at the cost of reducing the status of the other participants. After all, it is entirely possible that other participants have just as much cultural and linguistic knowledge as the interpreter (especially in business or government settings) but that their skills are being employed in a very different role. Interpreters surely bring something to the table that the other participants cannot provide while they are engaged in other work.

Indeed, the recurring and inherent dangers that arise when the role of the interpreter is over-emphasised might explain why the conduit model was so popular and remains so to this day. In any attempt to describe what interpreters do, we have to remember that they always do their work *with* others, not just *for* them. Without the speaker, interpreters have nothing to say; without the audience, they have no one to say it to; without the interpreter, the participants can say whatever they like but no one will understand any more than the bare minimum.

These complications and dangers mean that it is important to remember that both the triadic model and the conduit model are deliberate oversimplifications of interpreting. In the next chapter, when we try to figure out *how* interpreters do their work, we will look at some more complex models. For now, however, it is useful to take a step back and ask two key questions about the models and definitions we have seen so far:

1) Which model represents interpreting more accurately?
2) Which model is more useful for beating the bots?

Which model beats the bots?

I will admit that I am a big fan of the game Mario Kart. In that game, you race around a variety of gaudy tracks in cartoonish cars, driven by even cartoonier characters, and try to be first to the finish line. There's a catch, however. At various points around the track are spinning boxes with question marks on them. Drive over one of them and you are semi-randomly assigned a weapon. You and every other player can use those weapons to knock over the other cars, push them off the track, shrink them or do various other things. For the best racers, using weapons wisely is an integral part of their strategy.

What does that have to do with interpreting? If we are going to win the battle against the plethora of machine interpreting solutions that are gunning for our careers, we need to make sure that we are using the right tools for the job. We won't win just by driving ourselves at a faster pace. The most foundational tool we have is the way we think about our own work.

The conduit model might seem to be super-professional, but it reduces interpreters to a role that is unmistakably robotic.

```
Just say what the speaker said. Just say what the speaker
said. Commence coffee drinking. End coffee drinking. Go home.
```

It would be ironic at best to attempt to lure potential clients away from machine interpreting by saying that we are better conduits than they are. Technologically speaking, that can only be true for so long, as we shall see in Chapter 3.

The conduit model also idealises to the point of absurdity the realities of everyday interpreting. Interpreting is more complex than the conduit model because communication is more complex than the conduit model. Sometimes clients will look to us for the clarification of a term. At other times we will need to ask a client to pause so we can interpret. The fact that we are there in the room makes it impossible for us to suddenly become invisible (Downie, 2017).[2]

The triadic model, on the other hand, for all its weaknesses in terms of expressing why clients hire interpreters in the first place and all its dangers in overstating the role of interpreters, offers a much better platform. Instead of arguing that great interpreting is about disappearing into the background, the triadic model accepts that interpreting makes a difference and works out from that point. By putting teamwork and shared responsibility at its core, it not only elevates the position of the interpreter but emphasises their shared humanity too.

In the conduit model, interpreters process language; in the triadic model, they work with people to make meaning. In the conduit model, interpreters are equipment; in the triadic model, they are partners and participants.

If we want human interpreters to be seen as the gold standard, we can do a lot worse than making clients aware of the difference interpreting makes and their part in the process. Defining interpreting as teamwork implies that it is a very human occupation. Instead of seeing it as the flawless, impartial passing of preexisting meaning from language to language, the triadic model views interpreting as a process involving (at least) three parties with different backgrounds – all attempting to arrive at mutual understanding together.

Turning theory into practice

Much of the rest of this book is dedicated to turning ideas that might seem theoretical into practical, down-to-earth strategies. Underlying all of this, however, is the need for interpreters to present themselves as doing a job that is too human to be replaced by machines and too valuable to be underpaid. Rethinking our own models of interpreting is a vital part of that process.

So what does the practical outworking of a different model of interpreting look like? Applying a new model means many things, from redesigning interpreter PR (Chapters 4 and 10) and marketing interpreting on the basis of the difference it makes (Chapter 11) to developing ourselves to make more intelligent decisions that produce better results (Chapters 12 and 13). For the moment, however, it will suffice to ask one very simple question:

If you have a website, how do you describe what you do?

Almost every interpreter website I have seen has some section explaining what an interpreter is. It's a very useful page, especially given that many people don't know the difference between a translator and interpreter. Yet it can often be a very boring page.

How excited do we really think potential clients will be about reading the words "impartial" and "meaning"? How much attention will they really pay to details about different forms of interpreting and the equipment required?

Precisely because there are rivals presenting an alternative vision of interpreting, it is now vital for interpreters to think carefully about how they are presenting themselves and how client-friendly their communications are. If you have a website, it is worth reading your own writing and asking whether your presentation of interpreting implies that clients absolutely must hire a qualified human if it is to work for them.

While most of the chapters of this book will not end with questions or challenges, this one will. Here it is:

Go through your website, professional profiles, and social media feeds and look carefully at the picture you are painting of interpreting. Ask yourself whether your portrayal of your work makes you look like a well-oiled machine or a skilled partner and whether it is obvious why a computer could never replace you.

Notes

1   https://www.youtube.com/watch?v=cY_mqaWbKvs
2   That point also poses interesting questions about the uses and advisability of remote interpreting. That, however, is a question for another book.

References

AIIC 1999, 'Practical guide for conference interpreters', *aiic.net*. <http://aiic.net/p/628>.
Beaton, M. 2007, 'Interpreted ideologies in institutional discourse: the case of the European Parliament', *The Translator*, vol. 13, no. 2, pp. 271–96.

Clifford, A. 2004, 'Is fidelity ethical? The social role of the healthcare interpreter', *TTR: traduction, terminologie, rédaction*, vol. 17, no. 2. <http://www.erudit.org/revue/ttr/2004/v17/n2/013273ar.html>.

Dean, R. K. 2014, 'Condemned to repetition? An analysis of problem-setting and problem-solving in sign language interpreting ethics', *Translation & Interpreting*, vol. 6, no. 1, pp. 60–75.

Dean, R. K. and Pollard, R. Q. 2006, 'From best practice to best practice process: shifting ethical thinking and teaching', in *A new chapter in interpreter education: accreditation, research and technology: proceedings of the 16th national convention of the conference of interpreter trainers*, CIT, Monmouth, OR, pp. 119–32. <http://doc.wrlc.org/bitstream/handle/1961/10197/CIT2006.pdf?sequence=3#page=127>.

Downie, J. 2017, 'Finding and critiquing the invisible interpreter – a response to Uldis Ozolins', *Interpreting*, vol. 19, no. 2, pp. 260–70.

Napier, J. 2004, 'Interpreting omissions: a new perspective', *Interpreting*, vol. 6, no. 2, pp. 117–42.

Reddy, M. J. 1979, 'The conduit metaphor: a case of frame conflict in our language about language', *Metaphor and Thought*, vol. 2, pp. 164–201.

Roy, C. B. 1999, *Interpreting as a discourse process*, Oxford University Press, New York.

Seleskovitch, D. 1968, *L'Interprète dans les conférences internationales: problèmes de langage et de communication*, Lettres Modernes.

Seleskovitch, D. 1975, *Langage, langues et mémoire: étude de la prise de notes en interprétation consécutive*, Lettres Modernes.

Seleskovitch, D. and Lederer, M. 1984, *Interpreter pour traduire*, Pub. de la Sorbonne.

Shannon, C. E. 1948, 'A mathematical theory of communication', *Bell System Technical Journal*, vol. 27, no. 3, pp. 379–423. doi:10.1002/j.1538-7305.1948.tb01338.x.

Torres Díaz, M. G. and Ghignoli, A. 2014, 'Interpreting performed by professionals of other fields: the case of sports commentators', in *The second conference on Non-Professional Interpreting and Translation (NPIT2)*, Gemersheim, Germany. <http://dspace.uma.es/xmlui/handle/10630/8130>.

Turner, G. H. 2005, 'Towards real interpreting', in Marschark, M., Peterson, R., and Winston, E. (eds.), *Sign language interpreting and interpreter education: directions for research and practice*, Oxford University Press, New York, pp. 253–65.

Wadensjö, C. 1998, *Interpreting as interaction*. Longman.

Wilcox, S. and Shaffer, B. 2005, 'Towards a cognitive model of interpreting', in Janzen, T. (ed.), *Topics in signed languages interpreting: theory and practice*, John Benjamins, pp. 27–50.

Chapter 2

How humans interpret

How do you do it?

It's a question commonly posed to interpreters and one that has caught the imagination of psychologists, neurologists and interpreters themselves for almost as long as interpreting has existed. Anyone who gets even the slightest idea of the load the interpreters carry and the knowledge they need to have to complete even a basic assignment becomes fascinated by the fact that interpreting is even possible. So how do human interpreters do their job?

Sadly, this chapter can't give a final answer. In fact, even a provisional answer would take more than the rest of this book and would still have to include discussions of how much evidence is actually available and what it tells us. Instead of trying to go into the most minute details of research, I want to give an overview of some of the trends and models and methods in research on how we do our jobs. Despite all the work done on the mental and psycholinguistic processes used by human interpreters, there is still a big unanswered question about how human interpreters do their jobs, which we shall look at near the end of this chapter.

Modelling how humans interpret

It's the late 1950s. Conference interpreting is making its way to becoming a fully fledged, recognised profession. International organisations like the United Nations (founded in 1945), the European Coal and Steel Community (founded in 1952), NATO (founded in 1949) and the Council of Europe (also founded in 1949) are growing and gaining strength. At the heart of their success is the role played by this small but growing cadre of conference and diplomatic interpreters. The world that was amazed at the ability of interpreters to make the Nuremberg War Trials possible between 1945 and 1949 is now becoming increasingly reliant on them to provide the foundation for new kinds of international diplomacy.

Just at this time, when the first wave of international organisations had been founded and conference and diplomatic interpreting was growing apace, a researcher by the name of Eva Paneth completes her master's dissertation, often seen as the first MA to be completed in interpreting. Plainly titled "An Investigation into Conference Interpreting," her work, in the words of Franz Pöchhacker and Miriam Shlesinger, "anticipates many of the methodological quandaries which haunt and intrigue interpreting researchers to this day" (Pöchhacker and Shlesinger, 2002, p. 30).

Her most interesting findings, from the point of view of discovering how humans interpret, was that there is always a time lag between the speaker saying something and the interpreter giving their version, and that simultaneous interpreters did not really worry too much about avoiding speaking and listening at the same time. While they could make use of speaker pauses, they felt no real need to fit the interpretation of utterances into those rare moments when speakers stopped talking (Paneth, 1957 in Pöchhacker and Shlesinger, 2002, pp. 33–34).

While Paneth's dissertation covered a wide range of interpreting – from the aforementioned simultaneous interpreting to consecutive interpreting (ibid., pp. 36–38), commercial and military interpreting (ibid., pp. 38–39), *chuchotage* or whispered interpreting (ibid., p. 39) and telephone interpreting (ibid., pp. 39–40) – the vast majority of other work on the cognitive side of interpreting concentrates on simultaneous interpreting in conference settings. The reason for this is simple: simultaneous interpreting seems to be one of the most amazing feats of human intelligence.

Simultaneous conference interpreting also has another clear scientific benefit: to all but the most critical eye, interpreting in a laboratory looks very much like interpreting at a conference or large meeting. Interpreters can sit in similar booths to the ones they use at work, use equipment similar to what they use at work and, apart from one or two rather (in)famous examples (e.g. Dillinger, 1994), they can interpret the kinds of texts they would interpret at work. All this makes simultaneous interpreting seem like the ideal subject to study in controlled conditions.

It should be no surprise, then, that work on interpreter cognition – how interpreters think – and specifically interpreter cognition in simultaneous interpreting came to dominate early interpreting research. From David Gerver's exploration of the effects of speed and background noise on interpreting quality (Gerver, 1971) to Valeria Darò's (1989) study of memory and attention in simultaneous interpreting and even to the first release of Daniel Gile's seminal textbook *Basic Concepts and Models for Interpreter and Translator Training* (Gile, 1995), which contains his "effort models," it was taken for granted that examining the psycholinguistic or neurological aspects of interpreting could uncover how interpreters do their job, and by extension how they could do their jobs better and how students could be trained to interpret.

A vital part of this process was the development of sophisticated models of what exactly was going on in interpreter's heads. The complexity of these models varied widely. On the less complex end, there are Daniel Gile's now famous "effort models." While the most oft-quoted of these models is his model of simultaneous interpreting, his model of consecutive interpreting with note-taking provides a fascinating example of a researcher looking to use a cognitive under-standing of interpreting to explain the task. This model looks like this:

a) *Phase One: Listening and note-taking*
   Interpreting = L + N + M + C
   L   Listening and Analysis
   N   Note-taking
   M   Short-term Memory Operations
   C   Co-ordination

b) *Phase Two: Target speech production*
   Interpreting = Rem + Read + P + C
   Rem   Remembering
   Read   Note-reading
   P   Production (Gile, 2009, pp. 175–176)

In these models of the two stages of traditional consecutive interpreting with notes, Gile tried to break down the process into its component parts and define how they relate to each other. Combined with his view that interpreters are con-stantly working on the edge of their cognitive capacity (Gile, 1991, 1999) and so need to manage how much of their attention they give to each stage of the inter-preting process, these models proved to be a powerful tool for helping interpreters understand the challenges facing them as they interpreted and for giving them some ideas for adjusting their thinking to perform better.

An important first point to notice about this model is one that it shares with all models of how interpreters do their job. To make it possible to understand the model and use it, the researcher has to create a simplified, abstract view of what is going on. One single part of the model, such as "listening and analysis" hides a large number of individual operations. If any researcher were to attempt to map these out, the problem would be finding an easy place to stop. While it might be informative to map out the communication between individual neurons, such information is unlikely to help anyone interpret more effectively. Equally, while saying "you just do it" is pleasantly simple and makes interpreting look nicely inscrutable, it doesn't help much either.

It's important to understand, then, that all theories on how humans interpret are not just built upon data but on the subjective decisions of researchers about what the relevant variables are and the necessary level of detail. We will come back to this point when we look at a detailed model later. For now, however, it is important to root any discussions in how interpreters do their job in the fact that it is entirely possible and sometimes helpful to think through other variables and operations that could be included in each model and ones that could be left out.

Another important point to note about cognitive models of interpreting such as this one is that, despite any protestations to the contrary, such models always imply the ability to use them to predict interpreter performance. As a simple example, right after Gile posits this model of consecutive interpreting, he uses it to produce mathematical inequalities to predict under what conditions the interpreter will fail to produce high-quality consecutive interpreting, due to running out of processing capacity in their brain to do the task or having to dedicate too much of their attention to a single aspect (Gile, 2009, pp. 176–177).

In fact, the act of trying to explain how human interpreters do their job is closely linked to the task of trying to predict the conditions under which they will perform well or otherwise. While psychologists and psycholinguists might see in interpreting an intellectually stimulating way to probe human cognition (Chernov, 1979; Christoffels, De Groot and Waldorp, 2003; Hervais-Adelman, Moser-Mercer and Golestani, 2011); since a high proportion of interpreting researchers are actually interpreters or interpreter trainers, their interests will tend to be rather more practical and down to earth.

This means that the level of detail in models of how interpreters do their job will almost always be relatively close to the level of detail that can be concisely explained to a class full of interpreting students. Models of how we interpret will also stay quite close to the things that interpreters can control or manage consciously. For example, to go back to the Effort Models we saw earlier, it is interesting to note that every single component of the models, with the possible exception of the total cognitive capacity of the interpreter, pertains to an area of performance that interpreter can work on or manage.

We can, and should, work on building better listening and analysis, note-taking, production, short-term memory and note-reading skills. While some researchers and trainers might not be big fans of the idea of separating interpreting into sets of skills and working on them (e.g. Setton and Dawrant, 2016), it has a certain attraction for trainers and coaches. Building a model that supposes that interpreting relies on the management and development of these skills is therefore incredibly convenient, as it gives teachers and students something they both need – a map of ways to develop better interpreting.

None of this says anything about the accuracy or precision of cognitive models of interpreting. In an ideal world, researchers would be able to use experimental data to create a model of interpreting that is both empirically accurate and precise enough to use in teaching and skills development. If you ask certain researchers in interpreter cognition what they are working on, that is precisely what they are doing. Some might even say that they have already achieved it. Understanding the trade-off between precision and usefulness and the subconscious or even conscious preference for models that can be turned into teaching materials is, however, still important. It prompts us to remember two keys.

The first key is that no model can ever be perfect. There will always be a need for greater definition or deeper explanation or finer testing. The weakness of every model of simultaneous interpreting is the existence of dialogue interpreting or consecutive interpreting or, if we really want to push cognition researchers, we can ask how existing models can be adapted for sign language interpreting, as Sherman Wilcox and Barbara Shaffer (2005) did. Every single model ever created is subject to severe constraints in terms of the interpreting mode it applies to, the data it is based on and the predictions that it can make. That means that they can be prescient and reliable in, say, simultaneous interpreting between German and English in conferences but fall down flat when people try to apply them to sign language interpreting in a hospital.

The second key to understanding cognitive models of interpreting is *operationalisation*. Operationalisation is the academic term for actually figuring out what a word or phrase means in the real world and, more importantly, how to test it and do research on it. For example, if a machine interpreting device boasts that it provides "outstanding quality," we would be right to want to know what exactly they mean by "quality" and "outstanding" and exactly which methods they used to test those claims.

In the case of cognitive models of interpreting, the operationalisation problem is more subtle. Imagine you have invented an extremely detailed deep model of how interpreters interpret. For it to be a proper scientific model, it has to be tested. That means that, for every step of your model, it needs to be possible to test that your model works exactly the way you say it should. It has to be feasible to design a project that can probe every factor, every step and every process you map out. That becomes a real problem when people develop models like the one proposed by Barbara Moser-Mercer (2002, pp. 152–153).

This model is incredibly detailed in its description of the interpreting process, from the most basic tasks of recognising words to the most complex of piecing together sentence structure. That is both its strength and its flaw. It might seem obvious to argue that interpreters possess a system for checking whether a string of phonemes is a word, but as soon as this stage is made part of a model of inter-preter cognition it becomes vital to closely define what is meant by this stage and how to check it. Every detailed whole-process model ends up with the same issues, especially when it comes to psycholinguistic and semantic processes, such as checking that what is said makes sense. After all, a phrase that might not make sense in one context could be perfectly valid in another. Language is contextual and understanding what someone means can be as dependent on your knowledge of the situation you are in as it is on any grammatical and semantic processing.

Here is a simple example. I once interpreted at a conference where one of the speakers was trying to make everyone feel stronger and more powerful by adopt-ing a certain stance. He called it a "power pose." Whenever he called out "Get your power pose on," it made perfect sense, as people knew that he meant that we had to take the stance he had painstakingly explained earlier in the day. Needless to say, if a speaker had walked into the nuclear power station that I had interpreted in earlier that year and uttered those same words, their audience would have won-dered what on earth they were talking about! The sentence "Get your power pose on" had a specific meaning in a specific context.

All of us could come up with similar examples from our own practice. So much of the language that we and our clients use is defined and constrained and given meaning by the context in which it is said. Something has simple as "time for tea" said in different parts of the United Kingdom could mean anything from a fifteen-minute break to grab a hot beverage to a two-hour sit-down dinner with dessert, depending on where you are and who says it.

It would seem that interpreters deciding whether something makes sense is not so much about asking "Does that make sense?" but about asking "What sense does that make here?" While models of how we interpret have long taken into account the importance of our long-term memory and our knowledge of the wider world (Kohn and Kalina, 1996; Moser-Mercer, 2002), it is hard to model and test these parts of the interpreting process because everyone's world knowledge and long-term memories are different. The challenge of figuring out what goes on in an interpreter's head becomes even greater when that "world knowledge" includes offhand remarks made at the conference, running jokes, or shorthand ways of referring to discussions that happened previously.

How on earth would anyone examine how interpreters end up reusing phrases used by clients later on in a meeting? For example, I was once interpreting during a fisheries policy meeting. It turned out that more than one policy recommendation would depend on the numbers and location of *xenophyophores*, a type of single-celled marine organism. Tired of trying to say xenophyophores, one French delegate took to calling them "les xéno-n'importe quois" and the English-speaking delegation responded by naming them the "xeno-whatchama-callits," which is a pretty good English translation of the French. It led to some very fun interpreting but we interpreters – and the poor people taking notes – had to be careful to remember that a "xeno-whatchama-callit" was actually a xenophyophore and that the presence of these organisms was actually a very important consideration. A couple of offhand phrases said by clients had to be stored in the interpreters' memories, alongside not just their meaning but their importance to the discussion. "Xeno-whatchama-callit" didn't just mean "xenophyophore" and its French translation (xénophyophore) but it became a reference to an entire set of discussions.

It is very difficult to see how any experimental study of interpreting could find a way to model an interpreter's memory in terms of the storage and management of quirky client phrases. While "xeno-whatchama-callit" isn't exactly likely to become a frequent term in any meeting you will interpret this week, every context has its own equivalent of xenophyophores. In international organisations, we might come across "Schengen" used not just to refer to the Dutch town but to the dismantling of border posts across Europe and what that meant for politics, trade, travel and ideology. In a British university, a sign language interpreter will almost certainly need to understand the relevant meanings of "REF" in whichever meetings they find themselves. It could simply be a reference to the staff member needing to submit their research to be assessed as part of the Research Excellence Framework (often simply shortened to 'REF'), it could be an allusion to bureaucratic attempts to score academic output or it could be an explanation of how well the university is doing in research or even a reminder of the need for good career and writing planning. Sure, traditionally, we might just have expected that we could give some version of it and be done with it, but for us to even be able to string together a meaningful sentence, we need to actually understand what the speaker means in the specific context when they say "Get your power pose on" or "xeno-whatchama-callit" or "Schengen."

What did we learn from cognitive work on interpreting?

For all the problems with modelling and methods and for all of the limitations of results, given the focus on simultaneous conference interpreting, cognitive methods did bring some very important insights into interpreting. For a start, research moved from "personal theories" (Gile, 1990), such as the still under-tested "theory of sense" or "deverbalisation hypothesis" that interpreters somehow extract pure meaning from words and reassemble exactly the same meaning in the other language (Seleskovitch, 1968; Lederer, 1997) to more complex models of language processing and eventually to attempts to understand how interpreters process several different sources of information and meaning at once (Bühler, 1985; Seeber, 2017). This move, which is complicated to examine, due to older theories being used in later studies and ideas appearing early but only taking root much later, shadows the development of gradually more precise methods for examining how we think and the production of increasingly more reliable results.

From the early studies that helped to explain the importance of clear sound and the effect of speed on interpreter performance (Gerver, 1971) to modern work summarising the effects of remote interpreting on interpreting quality (Braun and Taylor, 2012) or explaining how interpreters combine visual and auditory information without being overloaded (Seeber, 2017), two clear themes have emerged.

The first is that interpreting in any context is a complex task, involving at the very least, the combination of grammatical, text structural, wider-world knowledge alongside memory management, task co-ordination, monitoring of our own output and the ability to self-correct. This complexity is generally accepted, whether we take the view that interpreters have a single maximum amount their brains can process and deal with (Gile, 1991, 2009) or whether we prefer the view that interpreters have separate mental resources available for different information sources (visual, auditory, etc.) (Seeber, 2017, p. 462) and so their capacity is spread out among several areas.

As research into interpreter cognition has developed, it has become very clear that interpreters do much more than simply listen to a strip of text and then look up the words in that text in some kind of brain dictionary. Interpreters can and do take into account the shape of a speaker's mouth, information presented on screens or in term lists, body language and the co-text of the rest of the speech they hear. While researchers are still far from explaining the exact methods interpreters use to do this, the fact that they do all this is firmly established.

The second theme is that, due to this complexity, the performance of interpreters is very sensitive. Alongside the result already mentioned on the effects of speed and sound quality, researchers have shown the difference that interpreting mode (Gile, 2001), the density of the source text (Plevoets and Defrancq, 2016) and the word order of the source text (Seeber and Kerzel, 2011), among many other factors, can affect the quality of the interpreter's output. It might not be that interpreters are always working at maximum capacity and so walking a tightrope (cf. Gile, 1999) between success and failure at any given point. There is sufficient evidence to show that however we are interpreting, there are a multitude of factors that can put us off.

What is safe to say from all the work that has gone on to understand how interpreters do their work is that they take in information from a wide variety of sources to clarify and augment what the source language speaker is saying or signing. Presented and managed well, this information actually aids processing and allows interpreters to decide what the sequence of words uttered by the speaker means and then, from that, to create a version in the target language. Strategies will vary from interpreter to interpreter (Isham, 1994) across different interpreting modes (Gile, 2001) and will also take into account the knowledge that the interpreter has of the people they are interpreting for (Napier, 2004). Interpreters also tend to feel they perform better when they can see how the audience is reacting and adjust their output to suit (Braun, 2013). This also means adjusting how they use pronouns rather than just saying the equivalent of "I" when the speaker says "I" (Angermeyer, 2015, pp. 82–90), adding in information that the audience may have forgotten (Karlik, 2010) or even explaining cultural references (Eraslan, 2011, p. 193).

Faced with the reality that the dynamics of interpreted events were far more complex than anything we could create in a laboratory, researchers soon found that it was vital to understand the contexts in which interpreters worked. That opening out of the research process would forever change the course of interpreting research.

From cognition to context

It's at this point that keen Interpreting Studies researchers will want to stop me in my tracks. The last three studies I mentioned, from Philipp Angermeyer (2015), Jill Karlik (2010) and Şeyda Eraslan (2011), are most definitely *not* studies of interpreter cognition, even if they do reveal some aspects of interpreter behaviour which do need to be examined in studies of how interpreters think.

If they aren't studies of how interpreters think, why do they appear in a section on interpreter cognition? These studies represent a wider wave of work, dating back to at least the mid-1990s, which challenged some of the preconceptions that lay behind both work on interpreter cognition and, more profoundly, behind our traditional approaches to interpreting.

In the 1990s, researchers such as Cecilia Wadensjö (1992) and Cynthia Roy (1992, 1999), followed closely by more theoretical discussions (Turner, 1995; Tate and Turner, 1997), examined real-life interpreted events and found that they bore little resemblance to what interpreting codes of conduct and research on interpreter cognition said interpreters should be doing. Instead of neutral, professionally distant mediators deverbalizing meaning and passing it along with just the right amount of cultural context, these scholars found and discussed interpreters coordinating who could speak, expanding on what was said and working with the other participants to figure out what was meant.

Faced with this surprising data, and in response to increasing interest in public service interpreting and community interpreting, a whole new way of researching interpreting arose. Instead of creating laboratory experiments, it became fashionable for interpreting scholars to go to interpreted events and record them, transcribing the data before combing through it for clues as to how the interpreters were relating to the other participants, what roles they were playing and what effects this was having on the events themselves.

Interpreting Studies has since discovered a whole host of new methods, from using corpora – collections of hours and hours of interpreted speeches – to including interviews, focus groups, online surveys and role playing. The essential division this created between viewing interpreting as largely a cognitive challenge, which can be understood through controlled experimentation and precise modelling, and viewing interpreting as a largely social practice that has to be observed where it occurs in real life, still persists.

Of course, it is not and probably has never been a matter of a strict dichotomy of the kind suggested by Anthony Pym (2008). Researchers did borrow from both sides, and most researchers today would accept that we need knowledge from both points of view to create a well-rounded view of interpreting. For the purposes of this chapter and for the rest of this book, however, it is important to understand how the shift from experimental research on interpreter cognition to observational research on interpreter behaviour in real-world interpreted events led to a corresponding shift in the way researchers saw interpreting, and it is worth noting that the reverberations and results of that are still being felt today. So what actually happened and why does it matter in the context of deciding whether human interpreters have a future? A helpful way of understanding all this is through the lens of one important researcher.

Why context changes everything

I had the pleasure of having Prof Ian Mason as one of the lecturers who led the Translation Studies module of my master's degree in Translation and Conference Interpreting at Heriot-Watt University. In fact, we were the very last class he taught before he retired. I do hope that the experience of teaching us had absolutely no effect on his decision at all!

A few years before I arrived at Heriot-Watt, he had edited a book with a rather cryptic title. This book, *Triadic Exchanges* (2001), looked at dialogue interpreting in a variety of settings, from students learning to interpret in the classroom to an Italian missionary interviewing a Confucian scholar in eighteenth-century Japan. The core theme of the book was that dialogue interpreting, when the interpreter is interpreting a conversation between two people who don't speak the same language, is most definitely not a process where the interpreter just says what each of the other people say. Like Cynthia Roy (1992, 1999) and Cecilia Wadensjö (1992, 1998) before them, the authors of each of the chapters in that book found that interpreters adopt a number of techniques to make meetings a success, techniques which are not always the ones typically taught in the classroom. How advisable and successful those techniques are was a topic of discussion in more than one of the chapters.

As I was attending the university to become a conference interpreter and not a community interpreter, I honestly felt that the dialogue interpreting classes I had to take and books on dialogue interpreting, like that one, were only tangentially relevant. Yet Prof Mason, himself mostly a scholar of translation specialising in text linguistics and discourse analysis, had decided to edit the book and freely discussed some of the ideas from it in his teaching. The fact that he had edited that book should actually have been no surprise, since he had suggested in an earlier book that context was the factor dialogue interpreters used most to understand and interpret what was going on (Hatim and Mason, 1997, p. 43).

Triadic Exchanges and earlier research showed that if we wanted to understand how dialogue interpreters do their work in hospitals, interviews, doctors' surgeries, universities, negotiations and the like, we need to understand how interpreters understand and use the contexts in which they worked. That made a lot of sense, but still, as a conference interpreter, I didn't see the relevance. I got stuck into linguistic devices like cohesion (how words and phrases are used to link sentences together), text genres and text structure. After all, Prof Mason had himself written that these were the most pertinent and accessible features of texts for interpreters working in simultaneous and consecutive interpreting with notes (Hatim and Mason, 1997, p. 43).

My attitude at that time reflected a division that was and is much sharper than the division between research on how interpreters think and the contexts in which they work. Even today, I come across interpreters – polished, experienced, professional, trained interpreters – who believe that there are some concerns that are exclusive to conference interpreting and some ideas that only work in community interpreting or public service interpreting. If one talks about interpreters being active participants and the context of the event affecting their work, some conference interpreters will still dismiss this idea in exactly the same ways as I almost did while I was doing my master's. "We're shut up in soundproof booths," they retort. "We're not nearly as involved as community interpreters," they argue. It makes sense that dialogue interpreters are actively involved in the events at which they work. Does that really apply to conference interpreters, who are several rows of chairs away from the speaker and whose only contact with the audience is mediated by some large infrared transmitters and headsets whose design is reminiscent of a 1990s personal cassette player?

I didn't know it when I was doing my master's, but there was a book in the library that had already shown that belief to be a myth and, while I was completing my studies, there was a PhD student in the same department whose work would provide enough evidence to completely dismiss it for good. The book had a title that could not be more academic-sounding if it tried. Ebru Diriker's *De-/re-contextualizing Conference Interpreting: Interpreters in the Ivory Tower?* (2004) might not have had the title of a Hollywood blockbuster, but its contents could and should have been the academic equivalent of one. It's influence on this present book is so powerful that discussion of it will return in Chapter 4.

The most stunning finding in the book was that there was a mismatch between what interpreters said they do and what they actually did in an assignment. While the interpreters tended to say all the right things about being neutral and saying only what the speakers said (Diriker, 2004, pp. 67–74), their actual performance was far more active, advising speakers (pp. 133–137) and adjusting the pronouns they used to distance themselves from certain content (pp. 137–144). It's worth bearing in mind that these interpreters were no amateurs. They were professional, trained interpreters with the same commitment to standards as anyone reading this.

The response to Diriker's book was surprisingly muted. One early and otherwise positive review fell back on the standard line that the book, like all interpreting research, had the weakness of "basing conclusions and hypotheses on a very small number of opportunistic samples" (Matthews, 2006, p. 155). This attitude prevailed despite the fact that researchers had been finding similar patterns in other forms of interpreting for over a decade by then, and there should have been little surprise in finding similar behaviour among conference interpreters.

What made Diriker's book so important is that it showed clearly that conference interpreters, at least those two interpreters, were as affected by the contexts in which they worked as were any other interpreter. As John M. Matthews correctly pointed out in his above-mentioned review, there was always a reason for interpreters stepping out of their normal role of using the same pronouns as the speaker. Perhaps a speaker was inaudible or there was a culture-specific idea that needed to be explained or even the speaker may have accused the interpreters of doing a bad job (see the discussion in Matthews, 2006, p. 153). Every shift away from the behaviour we might expect of interpreters was motivated by some external, contextual factor.

The kind of context-dependent interpreting found by Ebru Diriker also turned up in a thesis that was being written while I was studying for my master's. In her PhD thesis, Morven Beaton (later Beaton-Thome) analysed interpreting from German to English during three political debates in the European Parliament that took place during September 2001 (Beaton, 2007, p. 88). During these debates, she noticed that interpreters' familiarity with commonly used metaphors affected their output. They ranged from occasionally turning a metaphor into its literal sense – for example, occasionally substituting the phrase "European Union" when the source language speaker referred to the organisation as a "ship" – to using metaphors that were common in the speech of MEPs, such as seeing the enlargement of the EU as a race, even before the MEPs themselves did (p. 193).

In her view, it would seem, then, that the interpreters' decisions tended towards strengthening the power of the institutional ideology represented in the speeches (p. 194). Whether this was a deliberate political manoeuvre or simply a case of their familiarity with the environment – meaning that certain solutions were easier to find – is an open question. Even if it is the case that the interpreters found it easier to find certain solutions because they were the ones they were used to, that would simply be even more evidence that the decisions we take are affected by the contexts in which we work.

If interpreters working in as lofty a place as the European Parliament find their output affected by the context, then surely that is enough to suggest that the arguments for seeing interpreters as active participants in every event at which they work apply to every single interpreting setting. While the first decade of research that showed that interpreters are active participants in the events at which they work could have been dismissed as a quirk of dialogue interpreting, finding analogous patterns in the performance of professional conference interpreters and staff interpreters at the European Parliament should have been enough to convince everyone that something bigger was going on.

Needless to say, it wasn't. To this day, there are still some conference interpreters and indeed, some interpreters in other settings, who cling to the idea of interpreters as those who "just" say what the speaker said. Jump on any Facebook group for interpreters or even go to any conference where interpreters are attending and you will be guaranteed to find at least one interpreter who is scandalised by the idea that we should even think of ourselves as being involved in the events at which we work.

Yes, all this applies to court interpreting too!

For a while, the hardiest of the holdouts were spoken language legal and court interpreters. While sign language interpreters in just about every setting had long accepted the fact that they are active participants wherever they work, due to the powerful research of people like Robyn Dean and Robert Pollard (2001, 2004), Jemina Napier (2004; Napier and Barker, 2004) and Graham Turner (1995, 2005), spoken language court interpreters had been almost impervious to any attempts to see interpreters as anything but the objective, dispassionate relays of what the speaker said.

There are very good reasons for them to think so. As Anthony Pym points out in his rather challenging video "Spoken and written in conference interpreting, Part 1"(2012), one of the purposes of interpreting in most courts is to allow the creation of a monolingual written record of what was said in court. Yes, *we* might want to stress the human rights reasons for interpreting, but we can't ignore the fact that, in many jurisdictions, when the written record is made, the on-record words of the interpreter completely replace those of the person who does not speak the language of the court. We can either see this as the interpreter becoming a non-person and their speech being assigned to the minority language speaker or we can see this as the voice of the minority language speaker being erased and being replaced with the voice of the interpreter.

Either way, the fact that the on-record words of the interpreter are accepted as becoming the words of the minority language speaker for the sake of the written record places a certain amount of responsibility on the interpreter. Part of that responsibility is to say exactly what the speaker said, exactly how they said it. If the interpreter butts in with their own opinion or decides to make the speaker sound more eloquent or less educated, that would not be a faithful rendition of what was said and those words could sway the court.

For the complete and untarnished representation of the words of the minority language speaker to be seen as an achievable goal, everyone involved has to make some assumptions about the way that languages work and the way that interpreting works. These assumptions have become so fundamental to legal interpreting and especially court interpreting that to question them seems almost unthinkable. Since we are looking at how human interpreters interpret, and it is clear that this takes a lot of hard thinking, thinking the unthinkable is a fairly logical next step, I think.

The foundational assumption is that languages use the same structures, techniques and features to generate the same meanings. For the rules of court interpreting to make sense, a hesitation in English must mean the same as a hesitation in French, and Japanese has to use honorifics in the same ways and for the same purposes as Spanish. If it isn't the case that languages use the same features for the same purposes, then the rules of court interpreting actively disadvantage minority language speakers, because they will lead to their being understood.

Strangely enough, in a famous court interpreting study carried out by Susan Berk-Seligson (2002), this is precisely what happened. In simulated court hearings, jurors tended to view Spanish-speaking witnesses as less trustworthy when interpreters were instructed to use honorifics in the same way as the witness did. Far from being a bastion of fairness and faithfulness, it seems that assuming that features are the same across languages might actually put already vulnerable people at a disadvantage.

Linguists and interpreters alike could have seen that coming. We know from experience that the best way to interpret English intonation into French is to change the structure of the sentence. We also know that techniques and features that make someone sound intelligent and artistic in one language can make them seem opaque and evasive in another. The foundational assumption in court interpreting therefore creates a false sense of equivalence. It's a neat legal fiction that creates as many problems as it solves.

The logical result of this assumption is that accurate interpreting is interpreting that keeps as close to the structure of the original as possible. This is the interpreting equivalent of the old idea that "literal" translations are somehow more accurate than "free" ones – a myth that has been comprehensively debunked for a long time. Literal translation and literal interpreting that takes no account of the differences in how different languages work, are just as likely to generate inaccuracies and misunderstandings as free translation (Downie, 2009). The same applies to interpreting.

The myth that literal translations are more accurate leads on to the fiction that the smoother the interpreting is and the fewer the number of explanations, requests for clarifications or requests for sidebars to explain issues, the better the interpreting must be. If the interpreter's words are going to be written down to take the place of those of the minority language speaker, then it is more comfortable for everyone involved if these words sound and read as smoothly as possible.

While good court interpreters might indeed find that there are situations where smooth interpreting is possible and produces excellent results, the danger is that smoothness is not in itself an indicator of fairness or quality. Just because the interpreter is whizzing along at light speed doesn't mean that they are delivering effective interpreting. Sometimes, the very best interpreters earn that title because they are aware enough to see problems arising and find ways of solving them.

As an interpreter who has never practised in court, I am well aware that writing all this puts me in a position in which I may be criticised. Yet none of these ideas are my own. The superficiality of the foundations on which courts across the world have built their norms for interpreting has slowly been exposed by careful research. A fine example of this is a recent book by Philipp Angermeyer, *Speak English or What?*

Angermeyer studied interpreted small claims court cases in New York City and found two groups of interpreters. The first group, educated and inculcated into the norms of court interpreting, did exactly what the current standards said that they should do. This was especially evident in their decision to use exactly the same pronouns as whoever was speaking. If the speaker said the equivalent of "I" in their language, so did these interpreters. If the speakers said the equivalent of "we," so did the interpreters. This pattern persisted whether they were consecutively interpreting the cross-examinations of the minority language speakers or using whispered interpreting to interpret the testimony of the English-speakers. A second group of interpreters, however, switched pronouns during their simultaneous interpreting, indicating who the speaker was and who they were speaking about (Angermeyer, 2015, pp. 88–89).

Why would interpreters suddenly jump into saying "she said" or "the arbitrator says" when accepted practice says to simply use the same pronouns as the speakers? Among other factors, this shift allowed interpreters to clarify who was speaking about what, allowing the minority language speakers to better understand what was going on (p. 91). Some interpreters also adjusted how they interpreted according to the arbitrator on duty and the arbitrator's preferred method of running the hearings (pp. 93–94).

There might be serious concerns about the implications of the second reason for interpreters to change how they interpret, but the first reason shows up the problems with the standard approach to legal interpreting. If our accepted practices are making it harder for people to understand what is going on, perhaps it's time to change them.

As important as the debate around standard legal approaches to interpreting is in its own right, its importance in the context of understanding how interpreters think is that wherever we find interpreting, we find interpreters making context-based decisions, and we find events that are indelibly marked by their presence. If we want to understand how interpreters do their job, we need to begin from the point of recognising that their jobs go much further than processing individual excerpts of language and that even this language processing is much more complex and dependent on many more factors than we previously expected. Linking studies of interpreter cognition with studies of how interpreters respond to the contexts in which they work is not just a nice academic goal; it's a project that has the potential to revolutionise how we understand interpreting and how we train interpreters. The better we understand that link, the better the interpreters we become.

How do humans actually interpret?

The only safe answer to the question posed in this chapter is that we don't actually know. What we do know, however, is that interpreters marry together incredibly intricate and sophisticated cognitive processes with highly tuned social and situational awareness. We also know that interpreters, wherever they work, are anything but passive conduits for linguistic meaning. They are active negotiators of that meaning. They do this not just by performing some kind of lookup process, as if they were walking dictionaries, but by matching what was just said to the contexts in which they work, their knowledge of the speaker, their knowledge of the audience and their wider world knowledge. It's no wonder that, despite the incredible breakthroughs of over 40 years of research into interpreter cognition and almost three decades of work on understanding how interpreters relate to the contexts in which they work, there are still large holes in our knowledge.

It's important to remember, as we go through this book, that everything we know about how humans interpreting points to interpreting itself being a very human process. It involves judgment calls, drawing associations between different ideas, linking the current situation to the wider world, understanding culture and sometimes even having the people skills to manage speakers. I used to think that interpreting was all about language skills with some people attached; now I realise that it's all about people skills with language skills attached.

These demands are not unique to one setting, either. Before anyone tries to argue that this setting is different or that language is different, we have to remember one truth: interpreting is interpreting, no matter where it happens. A discovery in one setting is likely to have analogues in others. Yes, different language pairs present different challenges (de Pedro Ricoy and Shamy, 2017) but it is possible to find analogous challenges between different language pairs. Interpreting is interpreting.

Beyond all the deep models and methodological improvements, and underneath all the smart theorising and challenging results, lies an understanding that humans interpret by taking information from a variety of sources, both new and old, combining them to build a complete understanding of not just what is being said but what is going on. It's this idea of what is going on, in terms of understanding the point the speaker is trying to make, how it can be made clearly in the other language and monitoring how it is being understood that makes interpreting work. Anyone who wishes to create a system that can do what human interpreters do has to meet the challenge of recreating all of this combining of information sources, understanding of culture, knowledge of human emotions and behaviour, and smart decision-making. In the next chapter, we will take a close look at the ways that engineers and programmers have tried to create machine interpreting systems. As we read that, it's worth thinking hard about how closely their thinking matches what we know about human interpreting and how important any mismatch might be.

References

Angermeyer, P. S. 2015, *Speak English or what?: Codeswitching and interpreter use in New York City Courts*, Oxford University Press.

Beaton, M. 2007, *Intertextuality and ideology in interpreter-mediated communication: the case of the European Parliament*, Unpublished PhD Thesis, Heriot-Watt University. <http://www.ros.hw.ac.uk/handle/10399/2028>.

Berk-Seligson, S. 2002, *The bilingual courtroom: court interpreters in the judicial process*, University of Chicago Press, Chicago, IL.

Braun, S. 2013, 'Keep your distance? Remote interpreting in legal proceedings: a critical assessment of a growing practice1', *Interpreting*, vol. 15, no. 2, pp. 200–28. doi:10.1075/intp.15.2.03bra.

Braun, S. and Taylor, J. 2012, 'Video-mediated interpreting: an overview of current practice and research', in Braun, S. and Taylor, J. (eds.), *Videoconference and remote interpreting in criminal proceedings*, Intersential, Antwerp, pp. 33–68.

Bühler, H. 1985, 'Conference interpreting: a multichannel communication phenomenon', *Meta*, vol. 30, no. 1, pp. 49–54.

Chernov, G. V. 1979, 'Semantic aspects of psycholinguistic research in simultaneous interpretation', *Language and Speech*, vol. 22, no. 3, pp. 277–95.

Christoffels, I. K., De Groot, A. M. and Waldorp, L. J. 2003, 'Basic skills in a complex task: a graphical model relating memory and lexical retrieval to simultaneous interpreting', *Bilingualism: Language and Cognition*, vol. 6, no. 3, pp. 201–11.

Darò, V. 1989, 'The role of memory and attention in simultaneous interpretation: a neurolinguistic approach', *The Interpreter's Newsletter*, vol. 2, pp. 50–56.

Dean, R. K. and Pollard, R. Q. 2001, 'Application of demand-control theory to sign language interpreting: implications for stress and interpreter training', *Journal of Deaf Studies and Deaf Education*, vol. 6, no. 1, pp. 1–14.

Dean, R. K. and Pollard, R. Q. 2004, 'A practice-profession model of ethical reasoning', *Views*, vol. 21, no. 9, p. 1.

Dillinger, M. 1994, 'Comprehension during interpreting: what do interpreters know that bilinguals don't', in Lambert, S. and Moser-Mercer, B. (eds.), *Bridging the gap: empirical research in simultaneous interpretation*, John Benjamins, Amsterdam, pp. 155–89.

Diriker, E. 2004, *De-/re-contextualizing conference interpreting: interpreters in the ivory tower?* John Benjamins Publishing Company, Amsterdam.

Downie, J. 2009, *The end of an era: does skopos theory spell the end of the 'free vs. literal' paradigm? Pneuma Review: In Depth* (Online). <http://www.academia.edu/downlo ad/30862247/JDownie-EndOfAnEra.pdf>.

Eraslan, S. 2011, *International knowledge transfer in Turkey: the consecutive interpreter's role in context*, Unpublished PhD Thesis, Rovira i Virgili University.

Gerver, D. 1971, 'Simultaneous and consecutive interpretation and human information processing', <http://www.eric.ed.gov/ERICWebPortal/recordDetail?accno=ED084906>.

Gile, D. 1990, 'Scientific research vs. personal theories in the investigation of interpretation', in Gran, L. and Taylor, C. (eds.), *Aspects of applied and experimental research on conference interpretation.* Campanotto Editore, Udine, pp. 28–41. <http://www.google. co.uk/url?sa=t&rct=j&q=&esrc=s&source=web&cd=2&cad=rja&uact=8&ved=0CCc QFjAB&url=http%3A%2F%2Fwww.cirinandgile.com%2F1990%2520scientifresvsper stheory.doc&ei=88wrVa7yDMTiaPL9gdgF&usg=AFQjCNGwU9UqPyruvs79meTI seQ-88JzFQ&sig2=na9vLywAjx8SZZjLmgXmag&bvm=bv.90491159,d.d2s>.

Gile, D. 1991, 'The processing capacity issue in conference interpretation', *Babel*, vol. 37, no. 1, pp. 15–27.

Gile, D. 1995, *Basic concepts and models for interpreter and translator training*, J. Benjamins Publishing Company.

Gile, D. 1999, 'Testing the Effort Models' tightrope hypothesis in simultaneous interpreting-A contribution', *Hermes*, vol. 23, no. 1999, pp. 153–72.

Gile, D. 2001, 'Consecutive vs. Simultaneous: which is more accurate?' *The Journal of the Japan Association for Interpretation Studies*, vol. 1, pp. 8–20.

Gile, D. 2009, *Basic concepts and models for interpreter and translator training*, John Benjamins Publishing Company, Amsterdam.

Hatim, B. and Mason, I. 1997, *The translator as communicator*, Routledge.

Hervais-Adelman, A. G., Moser-Mercer, B. and Golestani, N. 2011, 'Executive control of language in the bilingual brain: integrating the evidence from neuroimaging to neuropsychology', *Frontiers in Psychology*, vol. 2, p. 234.

Isham, W. P. 1994, 'Memory for sentence form after simultaneous interpretation: evidence both for and against deverbalization', in Lambert, S. and Moser-Mercer, B. (eds.), *Bridging the gap: empirical research in simultaneous interpretation*, John Benjamins, Amsterdam, pp. 191–211.

Karlik, J. 2010, 'Interpreter-mediated scriptures: expectation and performance', *Interpreting*, vol. 12, no. 2, pp. 160–85. doi:10.1075/intp.12.2.03kar.

Kohn, K. and Kalina, S. 1996, 'The strategic dimension of interpreting', *Meta: Journal des traducteurs/Meta: Translators' Journal*, vol. 41, no. 1, pp. 118–38.

Lederer, M. 1997, 'La théorie interprétative de la traduction: un résumé'. *Revue des llettres et de traduction*, no. 3, 11–20.

Mason, I. (ed.) 2001, *Triadic exchanges: studies in dialogue interpreting*, St. Jerome, Manchester.

Matthews, J. 2006, 'Review of: Ebru Diriker (2004). *De-/re-contextualizing conference interpreting: interpreters in the ivory tower?*' *JoSTrans: Journal of Specialized Translation*, vol. 5, pp. 151–7.

Moser-Mercer, B. 2002, 'Process models in simultaneous interpretation', in Pochhacker, F. and Shlesinger, M. (eds.), *The interpreting studies reader*, Routledge, London, pp. 149–61.

Napier, J. 2004, 'Interpreting omissions: a new perspective', *Interpreting*, vol. 6, no. 2, pp. 117–42.

Napier, J. and Barker, R. 2004, 'Sign language interpreting: the relationship between metalinguistic awareness and the production of interpreting omissions', *Sign Language Studies*, vol. 4, no. 4, pp. 369–93.

de Pedro Ricoy, R. and Shamy, M. 2017, 'Retrospective protocols: tapping into the minds of interpreting trainees', *Translation and Interpreting*, vol. 9, no. 1, pp. 51–71.

Plevoets, K. and Defrancq, B. 2016, 'The effect of informational load on disfluencies in interpreting', *Translation and Interpreting Studies. The Journal of the American Translation and Interpreting Studies Association*, vol. 11, no. 2, pp. 202–24.

Pöchhacker, F. and Shlesinger, M. 2002, *The interpreting studies reader*, Routledge.

Pym, A. 2008, 'On omission in simultaneous interpreting. Risk analysis of a hidden effort.', in Hansen, G., Chesterman, A., and Gerzymisch-Arbogast, H. (eds.), *Efforts and models in interpreting and translation research: a tribute to Daniel Gile*, John Benjamins, Amsterdam, pp. 83–105.

Pym, A. 2012, *(1) Spoken and written in conference interpreting, Part 1 – YouTube*, Monterrey Institute of International Studies, USA, viewed 28 June 2019, <https://www.youtube.com/watch?v=lF8VXzEit2U>.

Roy, C. B. 1992, 'A sociolinguistic analysis of the interpreter's role in simultaneous talk in a face-to-face interpreted dialogue', *Sign Language Studies*, vol. 74, pp. 21–61.

Roy, C. B. 1999, *Interpreting as a discourse process*, Oxford University Press, New York.

Seeber, K. G. 2017, 'Multimodal processing in simultaneous interpreting', in Schweiter, J. W. and Ferreira, A. (eds.), *The handbook of translation and cognition*, John Wiley & sons, Hoboken, NJ, pp. 461–75.

Seeber, K. G. and Kerzel, D. 2011, 'Cognitive load in simultaneous interpreting: model meets data', *International Journal of Bilingualism*, vol. 16, 2, pp. 228–42.

Seleskovitch, D. 1968, *L'Interprète dans les conférences internationales: problèmes de langage et de communication*, Lettres Modernes.

Setton, R. and Dawrant, A. 2016, *Conference interpreting: a complete course*, John Benjamins Publishing Company.

Tate, G. and Turner, G. H. 1997, 'The code and the culture: sign language interpreting-In search of the new breed's ethics', *Deaf worlds*, vol. 13, pp. 27–34.

Turner, G. H. 1995, 'The bilingual, bimodal courtroom: a first glance', *Journal of Interpretation*, vol. 7, no. 1, pp. 3–34.

Turner, G. H. 2005, 'Towards real interpreting', in Marschark, M., Peterson, R., and Winston, E. (eds.), *Sign language interpreting and interpreter education: directions for research and practice*, Oxford University Press, New York, pp. 253–65.

Wadensjö, C. 1992, *Interpreting as interaction: on dialogue-interpreting in immigration hearings and medical encounters*, Linköping University.

Wadensjö, C. 1998, *Interpreting as interaction*, Longman.

Wilcox, S. and Shaffer, B. 2005, 'Towards a cognitive model of interpreting', in Janzen, T. (ed.), *Topics in signed languages interpreting: theory and practice*, John Benjamins, pp. 27–50.

Chapter 3

How computers "interpret"

It was an event of international importance. In April 2018, Tencent, one of China's leading technology companies, hosted its Boao Forum for leaders in technology and government. The centrepiece was the first live use of "Fanyijun," a fully automated simultaneous translation bot and transcription service. Their honoured guests waited eagerly to see and hear this breakthrough in human capabilities.

What happened next was heartening for interpreters and heart-breaking for Tencent. Instead of delivering a flawless performance, Fanyijun alternated between nonsense and the kind of odd translations that were associated with the early days of online Machine Translation. *The South China Morning Post*, Hong Kong's leading newspaper, covered the event with sympathy mixed with veiled criticism. *Slator.com*, a news outlet for the translation and interpreting industries, was less understanding.

Lessons were not learned. Later in the same year, iFlyTek, another Chinese technology company, would run into controversy as it was accused of passing off the work of a professional interpreter as the output of its newest machine interpreting tool. In the end, the story would become so muddled with claims and counterclaims and changes that it was no longer clear what actually happened. But yet again, machine interpreting would fail to live up to the hype.

But how does machine interpreting actually work? Just as interpreters need a deep understanding of their own work and what goes on in their heads, we can't hope to have an intelligent conversation about the pros and cons of machine interpreting unless we actually know how the systems work. This chapter won't go into the tiny details of individual algorithms since they change all the time, but it will cover the basic operating principles that guide machine interpreting, with an emphasis on the part that actually does the translation.

A basic map of machine interpreting

We looked at various diagrams that try to represent human interpreting in Chapter 2. When it comes to machine interpreting, we only need one. Machine interpreting is basically a three-stage process, where the machine has to decode spoken language into text that can be processed by a Machine Translation engine before passing that text to a voice synthesiser. That means that the process looks like this (see Figure 3.1).

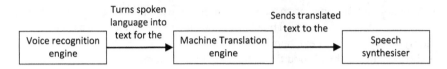

Figure 3.1 Basic operating model of machine interpreting.

On first glance, this diagram might seem very similar to the diagram of the conduit model of interpreting found in Chapter 1. That is no accident. The basic operating principles of machine interpreting are the same as those of the conduit model. Language is decoded, sent for processing and then encoded as a new sequence of language. For this reason you will often hear experts in Machine Translation and machine interpreting call translation a "sequence-to-sequence problem" – a phrase I first heard from translation technology consultant Tom Imhof at the BP18 conference but have since seen numerous times in books and articles.

Before delving any further into the details of how machine interpreting works, it is important to understand the assumptions that lie behind the current attempts to make it work. The principal assumption behind machine interpreting is precisely that interpreting is a sequence-to-sequence, conduit model problem.

Put in everyday language, machine interpreting designers see interpreting as nothing more or less than understanding one chunk of language and creating a new chunk in a new language that means the same thing. In this view, the social context in which the language is used, the reason for it being used and the people speaking are entirely irrelevant. All that matters are the words that are said.

In machine interpreting ... all that matters are the words that are said.

That might sound close enough to the way that some interpreters see their own job, but it conveniently dismisses some major social and grammatical issues. Imagine a machine interpreting from English where there is only one second person pronoun ("you") into a language where there are several, each marked for degree of formality, plurals and perhaps even social status. A decent human interpreter would be aware of the social requirements of the situation and would automatically pick the right pronoun to use; a machine is stuck with whatever is in its database. The best it might be able to do is to look at the rest of the sentence and see which pronoun tended to be used the last time it saw those words.

It is worth restating, then, that in machine "interpreting" there are only words and nothing but words. Any information not carried by those words cannot be taken into account. It is not an overstatement to say that machine interpreting is simply Machine Translation with audio. It therefore probably deserves to be called "speech translation" rather than anything that includes the word "interpreting." Machines don't interpret in the way we might think of humans interpreting; they transcribe, translate and then read out their answer.

Machine interpreting, or speech translation, as we will now call it, should be seen as a subset of Machine Translation and, for the moment at least, as being wholly dependent on developments in that field for any real improvements in quality. No matter how good the systems get at voice recognition and no matter how lifelike the synthetic voice output sounds, the hard limit on quality is found in the power of the Machine Translation engine used. In this chapter, therefore, I will concentrate on what interpreters need to know about the Machine Translation section of the process. Before that, however, it's worth briefly pausing to examine a recent article on speech translation that did point to some of the issues with the voice recognition part of the process.

Until *predictive* algorithms are found for voice recognition, the technology will always necessarily lag behind language use.

The beginning of the map – voice recognition

I was born and brought up in the West of Scotland. People have this strange idea that I have some kind of accent. Whether you agree with them or follow my argument that it's just everyone else who speaks funny, there is no doubt that being Scottish has one tiny problem. Voice recognition software still cannae git whit ah'm yabberin' aboot.[1]

That problem represents one of the main problems cited by the experts interviewed by Daphne Leprince-Ringuet for Wired UK, who were asked why speech translation gadgets performed so poorly. Matic Horvat, a researcher in natural language processing at Cambridge University, pointed out that "the quality of speech recognition degrades when you introduce it to things it hasn't heard before. If your training dataset is conversational speech, it won't do so well at recognising speech in a busy environment, for example" (Leprince-Ringuet, 2018).

Without good speech recognition, the translation engine can't do its job. As the old saying goes, "Garbage in, garbage out." For speech recognition to get the best results, you have to be using language it knows while speaking in a perfect environment for it to hear you. Toss it a few Glaswegian phrases while you sit in a pub with your mates or ask it to understand a noisy factory tour, and the rest of the process will fall down, too.

In the same Wired UK article, Daniel Gleeson, a senior analyst in consumer technology, pointed out that the only way to improve voice recognition is to continually gather more data on "specific accents, colloquialisms, idioms, all of which are highly regionalised" (Leprince-Ringuet, 2018). Speech recognition is immensely powerful and immensely data hungry. As language changes, the systems need to be trained again so they still work adequately.

There can be no doubt about how useful voice recognition is, and it will only get better. While in less technologically advanced days, I have had to hand over the phone to my wife so she could use her English accent to get through voice-activated call centre menus, the chances are that those days will be over at some point soon. As the big data companies suddenly take notice of the needs of Liverpudlians, Texans and Glaswegians, those voice-activated menus will get better at telling a "one" from "what?" The data to pull off such a feat will likely come from the growth in voice-activated digital assistants, such as Alexa and Siri.

This all sounds very hopeful, but until *predictive* algorithms are found for voice recognition, the technology will always necessarily lag behind language use. Teaching it to recognise "deproblematise" or "flexitarian" as words will involve the same process of repetition and guesswork as it does now.

Once we get over the need to constantly add new words and idioms, there is still another problem. For the moment, speech recognition systems simply concentrate on recognising words. Important details like intonation, stress and tone are entirely outside of their abilities. In some languages, that might not be too much of an issue, but in a language like English, where "I only told her I loved her" can take on seven different meanings, according to where the stress falls, that can be problematic.

In terms of pure semantics and grammar, nothing changes in that sentence when the stress moves. Yet a shift in emphasis changes the focus of the sentence, and interpreters normally pick up on such shifts and adjust their output accordingly. It's very common for interpreters into French to restructure their output to match the stress patterns of the English, for example. Such subtle nuances become all the more important in contexts such as courts, negotiations and counselling where tiny shifts in emphasis can mean success or failure, jail or freedom.

Assuming that your accent is compatible with voice recognition and you use words that are in its database, your spoken language – minus any intonation – is then turned into data that can be passed to the Machine Translation engine. It's at that point that the process begins in earnest.

Machine Translation – the brains of machine interpreting

Machine Translation – it's one topic that is sure to light up a room full of translators. It makes some professionals plan to pack up their bags and ride off into the sunset, while others look around for local pitchfork retailers to try to chase it out of town. There simply isn't enough room in this book, or any book, really, to discuss in detail all the different points of view or where Machine Translation might be going. For now, the most important thing is simply to understand two things about Machine Translation (which I will now start calling MT). We need to know how MT works and how the quality of MT is usually measured, since those quality measurements lie behind the majority of the claims made about speech translation.

Although there are three approaches to MT, only two seem to be in common use nowadays. The oldest and now rarest approach to MT is called Rules-Based MT (RBMT). The idea behind RBMT is that programmers and linguists work together to generate rules for each language, covering parts of speech, morphology, syntax and the rest. These rules are combined with bilingual glossaries.

To translate a text, the system first analyses each individual sentence of the source text according to the rules it has been given. Next, it works through the translation of each word root and the translation of each grammatical structure, including any prefixes and suffixes. This in turn is followed by a final stage, where the system attempts to fix any errors (Sreelekha, Bhattacharyya and Malathi, 2018, pp. 663–665).

The strength of RBMT is that it builds on the aggregated expertise of linguists in the rather daunting task of deconstructing the structures of one language and building a text in a new one. Suddenly, diagramming sentences becomes a vital life skill and arguments over present participles and gerunds seem worthwhile.

The problem with RBMT is that knowing your gerunds from your present participles isn't enough to translate well or accurately. Language users break linguists' nice, neat rules all the time, and every time language use changes, RBMT systems need to be adjusted. This, alongside the long-standing problem of dealing with idioms and ambiguity in RBMT, explains why most of the worst MT mistakes date from the days when RBMT dominated. Knowing a lot of linguistic rules is helpful, but if the system doesn't understand how words are used or when language is metaphorical, it will soon get into trouble. The discovery that it is important to know how language is actually used, and some impressive strides in processor and storage technology, brought about the next big shift in Machine Translation – Statistical Machine Translation (SMT).

If RBMT represents an idealistic view of language that is guided by rules and grammar, SMT represents an attempt to deal with the sheer muckiness and complexity of language. In SMT, what matters is the ways people actually use a language and not so much the rules of how it should be used.

For anyone who has studied linguistics, this split between language rules and language use should be familiar. It's very much the same distinction as linguists discuss when that talk about *langue* vs *parole* and competence vs performance. RBMT is very much on the *langue* and competence side of idealism and underlying structures, while SMT is firmly on the *parole* and performance side.

So how does SMT work? Figure 3.2 presents a small cartoon that demonstrates the basic principle.

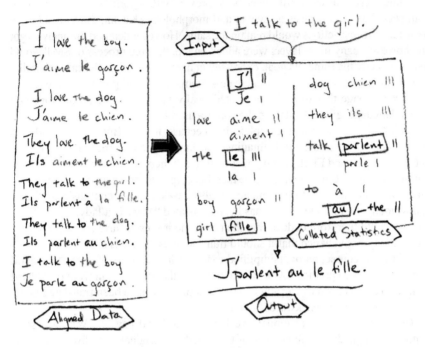

Figure 3.2 "Cartoon Theories of Linguistics Part IV—Statistical Machine Translation,"
© Trey Jones, *Speculative Grammarian*, Vol CLII, no. 4., used with permission.

Amidst all the discussions of language models, translation models and statistical indicators, the most important thing for us to understand about SMT is
that it works more or less as the comic suggests. To build an MT system, you
need to collect lots of aligned data, containing translations between the two
languages you are interested in, with each source text sentence aligned with
its target text translation. You also need lots of original language data in the
target language.

Within the aligned data, you look for patterns. To begin with, scientists used
to look for these patterns at the level of individual words. Which word or words
are most used to translate the word "I" or the word "boy"? Eventually, as you
might have guessed from the rather odd look of the output suggested in the cartoon, emphasis moved away from individual words to clusters. These clusters
would not always be the same as the usual phrases and clauses used in classical
linguistics. Quite the opposite, in fact. Since, as Franz Josef Och (2002, p. 9)
would argue, "the relationships between linguistic objects such as words, phrases
or grammatical structures are often weak and vague," the proponents of SMT
would devise their own clusters, based on whichever number of words provided
the best statistical results using the least processing power.

While these clusters would later be improved with algorithms that could deal with such little annoyances as syntax and morphology (Koehn, 2009, p. 11), the basic text and restrictions would remain the same. However detailed the analysis got and however many more layers were added on top, the core process of SMT would remain exactly the same. Its goal, expressed in many layers of statistical probability and mathematical notation, was to create systems that could generate sentences in a target language that were the most statistically likely translations of those in a source language, given the data in the corpora used for training the system.

If that all sounds rather complex, it's because it was. But the basic idea is simple enough to understand. Imagine you have a giant corpus of translations between French and English and you look through them to see how "Marie est une femme" has been translated. Imagine that this corpus is rather special and you can find 1,000 translations of this sentence. In 999 cases, it has been translated "Mary is a woman," and in one case, it has been translated "Mary is a lady." Your SMT engine would therefore deduce that the next time it sees "Marie est une femme," there is very high chance that it should translate it as "Mary is a woman."

That is, of course, an oversimplified case, but it will do to express the general idea. SMT tries to predict how it should translate the text it has in front of it based on how previous texts of varying degrees of similarity have been translated in the past. It is necessarily backwards-looking.

The complexity and continual tweaking of SMT did pay off. With access to almost unimaginably large corpora of translated and original texts from many different languages, due to the generosity of international organisations such as the UN and EU, the creators of SMT systems had access to the volume of training data that their systems needed. Assuming that the texts and translations were of sufficient quality – and that would be an assumption that should be safe enough, given the sources they tended to use – the resulting translations should be excellent too.

Depending on the particular case, they were. Any text in closely related languages that was in a field covered by the corpora could be translated to decent levels of accuracy. It would take more than this book to give a detailed account of the actual results found, although we will pause later to look at how Machine Translation quality is evaluated, but one interesting result stands out.

In a study that aimed to test the assumption that Machine Translation was always worse than the work of humans, Rebecca Fiederer and Sharon O'Brien asked 11 raters to rate 30 source sentences, three translated versions and three post-edited MT versions, for clarity, accuracy and style (Fiederer and O'Brien, 2009). Whenever you see or hear about experiments like that, it is important to think first about the results you expect to see. Most readers of this book would surely think straightaway that humans should win every time in this test against post-edited Machine Translation.

Sometimes, research throws up unexpected results, and this fact applies to the experiment just cited. The highest marks for clarity and accuracy went to machine translated and post-edited output. The human translators only won when it came to style and when the judges were asked to pick their favourite sentences (Fiederer and O'Brien, 2009, p. 52). Yes, it's important to remember that post-editing Machine Translation is done by humans, so this isn't a perfect human vs machine test. Yes, we can have long arguments about the qualifications of the evaluators and the usefulness of rating individual sentences, but the results are what they are.

We can argue back and forth all we like, but that will not stop the evidence showing that SMT can produce some good work that gets even more useful once humans have tidied it up. We might not like SMT. It might be poorly suited to certain languages and certain kinds of texts, but it is far from being useless.

Yet the Fiederer and O'Brien test cannot be directly applied to speech translation. In MT, the presence of words on a screen makes it possible to do all kinds of correction and editing between the computer producing its best guess and the text reaching a reader. This "post-editing." which is likely to become the mainstay of professional Machine Translation for most paying clients, simply can't apply to interpreting. The timescales required for interpreting mean that all you can ever hear is the raw, unvarnished output from the Machine Translation engine. Since SMT relies heavily on predictability and on high frequencies of the words and phrases it looks for, the creativity, messiness and sheer variety of spoken language might present a barrier.

There have been many improvements to the algorithms behind SMT, and the corpora that the systems can draw on are growing all the time. It is also becoming more common, with the advent of the open source Moses toolkit for Statistical Machine Translation (Koehn et al., 2007), for people to build their own specialist MT systems. Where organisations need translations of documents that are very linguistically similar, they can have MT churn them out rather than asking human translators to redo the same thing over and over again.

Since this book is about interpreting, it's worth thinking through the strengths and weaknesses of having an interpreting system that works on the basis of SMT. Surprisingly, the pros and cons are pretty easy to work out.

SMT is very good at spotting phrase-level patterns and matching them with their typical translations – in fact, that is essentially all it does. In the context of interpreting, that makes it reliable at conversations where the phrases used are common in print. In closely related languages, SMT-based speech translation will probably fare well when faced with someone asking directions, ordering a meal, or going to the pharmacy to get some painkillers. The exceptions to this rule would be that SMT will always deal with culture-specific terms (for example, the name of a certain church) in the way that they are frequently dealt with in the corpus. It is unlikely to supply the helpful information that, if someone in England tells you to turn right at the Dog & Duck, you should be on the lookout for a pub and not for a canine taking a bird out for a walk.

Even the contents of a typical chairman's introduction to a conference is likely to be handled fairly well by most SMT-based systems. As any interpreter in Scotland will tell you, the opening of a conference in Edinburgh will almost certainly involve thanking the organising team, ironic assurances that it doesn't always rain that much, details of the upcoming *ceilidh* and the promise of a whisky tour. A few minutes on Google would be enough to dredge up a few speeches in that vein, and since the patterns, jokes and lies about Scottish weather basically never change, it will be entirely possible to train an SMT engine to relay them.

While SMT is excellent at finding translations to existing phrases, it isn't built to determine what they actually mean or what tone they should be uttered in. It also entirely lacks any cultural sense or world knowledge. A simple example was discussed by Chris Taylor of the online news website Mashable who pointed out that in 2012, four years after Barack Obama became president, Google Translate was still turning the French phrase "le président américain" [the American President] into "Bush" (Taylor, 2012). Since it had more documents in its database which linked George W. Bush to the US presidency, it made perfect mathematical sense to keep the pattern going, never mind that the world had changed.

Efforts have been going on for some time to resolve this problem, and with IBM having already built a system that could beat humans at the knowledge-based game show *Jeopardy!* as early as 2011 (Best, 2013), it would seem that the problem could be solved. Yet answering game show questions is quite far from applying world knowledge to translation. Even if a computer knew that the Dog & Duck was a pub, it would still need to decide when and how and if to use that information in its translation and interpreting.

In short, SMT is very good at ensuring consistent translation of established patterns of text but elucidating their meaning or tone is beyond its abilities. The clarity and quality of its output also depends rather heavily on the quality of the data it has available. Using an SMT engine that was trained on diplomatic and scientific texts to provide interpreting at a European Works Council or a medical appointment will always produce less than stellar results.

But recently, SMT has been challenged by a newcomer. Rising from being a rare and rather exotic approach as recently as 2015 to being the dominant approach by 2017 (Koehn, 2017, p. 6), Neural Machine Translation (NMT) has been lauded for producing results that seemed impossible even a few years ago. But how does it work?

Before any description of the nuts and bolts of NMT, a few things need to be made clear. NMT is to Machine Translation what quantum physics is to the physical sciences. It's powerful, gives interesting results and seems to be the state of the art in terms of human knowledge, but it is almost impenetrable, even for its most knowledgeable experts. Physicists like to joke that the more you know about quantum physics, the less you understand it, and the same is true of NMT: there are parts of it where even the experts admit that they don't understand what is going on.

To understand NMT, we first need to understand the concept of machine learning. To understand deep learning, it helps to start with a rather simple problem: winning at noughts-and-crosses (tic-tac-toe to American readers).

Anyone over the age of about five understands the basic idea of noughts-and-crosses and the strategies needed to win or at least draw. Simple tricks, such as taking the centre, or winning two diagonally-opposite corners, and making sure you place a symbol in any space where your opponent could complete three in a row, make it a very easy game to programme a computer to play. In fact, when I studied Computing in Secondary School, one of our assignments was to write a programme that could do just that.

Creating a programme that contains all the rules and known tactics is the noughts-and-crosses equivalent of building an RBMT system. You tell the machine what the rules are and which patterns to look for and assume that the game includes enough of these patterns for it to perform well. In a small, tightly regulated game such as noughts-and-crosses, this is pretty easy and produces reliably good results.

Another way to programme a computer to play noughts-and-crosses would be simply to feed it all the possible games of noughts-and-crosses, all 255,168 of them (excluding symmetry and rotation), and then instruct it to run statistical analyses on them to find patterns. That would be fairly similar to the SMT approach to Machine Translation, except that the total number of sentences in a language is so big that you couldn't possibly get them all in. Instead, you have to use reduced sets, or "corpora."

The machine learning approach is different again. First dreamt up by computer scientist Donald Michie in 1961 when computing itself was still in its infancy, the machine learning approach to noughts-and-crosses ironically doesn't need any computers at all. All you need to do is to get 304 matchboxes, each with a different possible game position, and drop a number of coloured beads into each box, with each possible move in a given position being represented by a different coloured bead.

Starting with an empty board, the operator shakes the box representing the empty board position and pulls out a bead, the colour of which tells them where the system will play its first move. After the opponent moves, the operator then goes to the matchbox that corresponds to the current game position, shakes it and pulls out another bead. The process then repeats until the game ends.

If the system loses, then the beads of that colour remain out of their boxes, reducing the chance of that particular move being played again. If it wins, three more beads of the same colour are placed into the box for each move it made. If it is a draw, the beads are just returned to the boxes they came from. Once that is done, a new game is started, with the same process as before.

Over time, such a system will "learn" to make better moves, since they are given greater weight by the introduction of more beads. Conversely, it will also "learn" to make fewer bad moves, as they are punished by having beads removed. The important point, then, is that the results of one run are immediately fed back into subsequent runs to improve performance.

In its first outing, such a system could draw with humans most of the time after as few as 20 games. When it was built again in 2017 by a team of mathematicians on YouTube (https://www.youtube.com/watch?v=R9c-_neaxeU), it achieved similar results. A simple machine, with no living parts therefore "learned" to perform a well-defined task to a level where its performance rivals or beats that of humans.

The use of scare quotes around the word "learn" is deliberate and needs to be kept in mind as we explore the way that NMT works. If we define learning as the ability to use previous performance at a task to improve subsequent performance, then our pile of matchboxes and any computer system can learn. Yet that learning is limited. When a human learns, the learning from one task, say, picking up toys, can be applied to later, more complex tasks, such as carrying boxes, doing the dishes, or even eating. What seem like discrete skills are combined to accomplish more complex tasks. A human who knows how to eat a slice of carrot will soon apply that to eating a crisp or a chunk of sausage. Learning to hold a chunk of carrot turns into holding a pen, which turns into making marks on paper, which turns into writing, which turns into books.

Learning for humans is not just about successfully completing a single task but is about linking together knowledge and skills gained across a wide variety of different areas by different means (Siemens, 2005). However, when computing experts talk about "machine learning," they are referring to the ability of a system to take into account previous results to get better at a specific task. That means that machine learning can improve the performance of Machine Translation but cannot be used to teach an NMT system to make coffee or pick up children's toys. Similarly, machine learning can be used to improve the results of systems that can list all the elements of a picture but it can't turn that system into a replacement for an interior decorator.

Even within one task, the model used will determine exactly what improvement looks like. Machine learning can be used to tune NMT systems to score highly in certain quality tests, but the usefulness of that depends on how good the tests are in the first place. All machine learning systems are therefore tuned to perform a very specific task according to a strict set of success criteria.

So with all that in mind, how does NMT actually work? Underneath all the algorithms and fancy maths, basically, NMT systems use patterns or features in language to predict the next word in a sequence. One such pattern is words that tend to be used in similar contexts, or "word embeddings." NMT language models are therefore trained to spot such patterns and take them into account (Koehn, 2017, pp. 33–36).

Like SMT systems, NMT systems are trained on existing translations and on existing single-language corpora. From these, they build up a representation of how individual words are used, the words that tend to surround them and how these map to target language translations. NMT represents a step change from previous models of Machine Translation, as neural networks combine patterns together to look for wider trends and progressively improve by being able to incorporate the results of previous attempts into future work.

Since the basic principles of this latter, machine learning stage, were already explained above in the example of teaching a set of matchboxes to successfully play noughts-and-crosses, it is worth pausing for just a little while to understand how NMT systems can spot and use new kinds of patterns.

In NMT, as in all neural networks, calculations are done in artificial neurons. These are simply mathematical functions that take some input, run a calculation and produce an output. In neural networks, these artificial neurons are connected together so that the output of one artificial neuron becomes the input for the next and so on. Given the right functions and with the right representations of the input data, neural networks can do complex calculations, such as which words appear together more often and how this relates to their likely translations into another language. Add on the possibility of the machine adjusting these functions according to the results from each run, and the result is a very powerful way of doing translation, which tends to produce more fluent output than any other method currently available (see Koehn, 2017 for a detailed introduction).

There is no doubt that NMT is an incredibly powerful technique, but it does have several disadvantages, especially when applied to interpreting. The first and most basic is that, in common with other forms of MT, NMT can only take into account the co-text of a word, it cannot deal with social context or intention. When I interviewed Machine Translation expert Tommi Niemanen for this chapter, he pointed out that one solution to this problem is to tag language with a specific domain, such as pharmaceuticals or law. This should lead to any NMT system giving data from specialist corpora priority when it comes to translating specialist texts, yet interpreters will soon realise that there is a huge difference between giving priority to a set of data and recognising irony, much less being able to competently deal with it in a live speech.

If this seems to have shades of the debates between the conduit and triadic models, it should. Fundamentally, all MT models are built on the assumption that translation and interpreting can be carried out using the conduit model. The aim of the Machine Translation part of any speech translation system is not to produce new texts for a specific purpose but, to quote the interview with Tommi Niemanen for this book, "learning in NMT means that the system has maximised the error function." NMT is about optimising mathematical equations, not language as an interpreter would recognise it.

That leads to the second weakness of speech translation when applied to speech translation. Since MT algorithms are purely mathematical, it is not at all clear how they can learn in interpreting scenarios. In Machine Translation, quality is often measured using metrics such as BLEU scores, which compare the words used in machine-produced translation with those found in model translations made by humans. The closer the machine gets to that version, the better it is deemed to be. A further quality measure is to ask human raters to score the accuracy of individually translated sentences.

While it's true that debate about the usefulness of those quality metrics is now going on in the Machine Translation community (Läubli, Sennrich and Volk, 2018; Toral et al., 2018), their usefulness in speech translation is even more doubtful. To risk stating the obvious, interpreting produces spoken or signed texts, not written texts. Measuring quality in interpreting is a problem that still evades experienced researchers. Acknowledging the now obvious gap between client evaluations and interpreter perceptions (Gile, 1990; and see the discussion in Downie, 2015) simply adds on another layer of complexity.

What would it even mean for a speech translation to have produced good interpreting? Standard levels of linguistic accuracy risk a return to the failed conduit model and mean deliberately forgetting that interpreting does not exist simply to produce linguistic equivalence. Asking interpreters to rate output poses professional issues and requires researchers to forget that interpreting is not produced for interpreters. Lastly, taking soundings from interpreting users would be problematic as the very reason they need interpreting is that they don't understand the source language.

If a Machine Translation system is only as good as the data used to train it and the metrics used to evaluate it, then speech translation has many difficult problems to face before it is ready to come even close to replacing humans. Perhaps its biggest weakness, however, is the continued reliance on conduit model thinking, which leads to assuming that gluing a Machine Translation engine to voice recognition and voice synthesis is enough to produce good interpreting.

As unimportant as it might seem now, given the imposing challenges faced by the voice recognition and Machine Translation parts of the process, it's worth a short look at voice synthesis.

Speech synthesis

After all that, we come to the very last step of the process of speech translation: speech synthesis. At this point, the computer or app takes the written Machine Translation output, matches it with recordings of words, phonemes or even entire phrases from its database, smooths it all together, adds its best guess at intonation and produces an output.

Just like Machine Translation, it would take another entire book to explain in details how this works. To better understand the relevance of this process for speech translation, it helps to look briefly at some challenges. The first and most daunting is that, to quote speech synthesis researcher Marian Macchi (1998, p. 318), "[T]ext is an impoverished representation of a speaker's verbal intentions." Written words by themselves give only ambiguous cues as to how they should be said.

A simple example is the word "read" in English. Is it a present tense and therefore rhyming with "bead" or a past tense, rhyming with "bed"? What about the phrase "SAD isn't just about being sad" or "52 St. John st."?

In all of these examples, there is a word or cluster that is read more than one way. For humans who know that "SAD" is the acronym for "Seasonal Affective Disorder," it is not hard to disambiguate and reading those sentences aloud would not be a problem. For a computer to process those phrases and produce sensible output, it needs some way of working out when to spell out letters individually and when to treat an acronym as a word, when "st" means "saint" and when it means "street" and, of course, when "read" is in the past tense and when it is in the present.

Like Machine Translation, attempts to resolve these difficulties have tended to follow a similar trend of starting with rule-based approaches, moving on to statistical analysis and, more recently, neural networks (Lemetty, 1999, pp. 9–10; Dutoit, 2013, pp. 122–123). All of these approaches assume that the text is, in itself, sufficient to be able to work out how to pronounce words and how to use intonation and prosody.

The aim of all speech synthesis is therefore to produce output that sounds natural and is clear (Dutoit, 2013, p. 195) to the point of being indistinguishable from a human voice. This explains why it has found such an important use in assistive technology for people with vision difficulties and even among some translators, who find it helpful to have their translations read back to them to check for errors.

It still remains to be seen how helpful the current speech synthesis methods are for interpreting. While straightforward sentences, such as "Welcome to our lovely city" would not be likely to pose any real issues, many interpreters have found themselves in the difficult situation of trying to work out how to reflect the intonation and emphases of the source language speech in their target language version. The precise emphasis used in the sentence "I never said I was with him" could be important in a wide range of medical and legal contexts. Similarly spotting the small but important tonal and facial markers of irony, sarcasm, understatement, and play-acting can be a common, if not always welcome, job for conference interpreters.

Once again, it would seem that wider social, political, legal, cultural and geographical contexts are as important for understanding what speakers are trying to communicate as the actual words they use. How far speech synthesis can produce not just intelligible but correct and appropriate output without these cues remains to be seen.

A summary

It is helpful to wrap up this chapter with a short summary of both the current state of speech translation technology and possible future trajectories. We have seen that bringing together speech recognition, Machine Translation and speech synthesis promises to produce excellent interpreting but tends to fail at the task when put into real-world settings. For speech recognition, the main weakness is the need for large training databases, which need to be constantly added to as language shifts and new accents are introduced to the system. Speech recognition, while very powerful, is always necessarily backward-looking, relying on the speech samples that have already been analysed in order to decide how best to decode incoming speech.

For Machine Translation, recent technological shifts have indeed led to considerable progress when quality is measured using a small set of measurements. How well these measurements match with anything that actual users of interpreting might see as "quality" is up for discussion. Since all Machine Translation algorithms were designed for written texts, they also depend on large corpora to produce high-quality output and are only as good as the data put into them. Despite recent movements to improve performance, all MT systems are largely limited to the information found in the texts fed into them and cannot independently read the social contexts of the texts they handle, causing subtle but still important weaknesses.

Speech synthesis is the last step in the process. Here, the challenge has been to figure out how to pronounce words that are written identically yet said differently, as well as how to handle abbreviations and acronyms and decide on the correct intonation. Since currently no intonation information is passed on from earlier stages, speech synthesis systems can only decide on intonation on the basis of the written text passed from the Machine Translation part of the process.

In short, the greatest challenge facing speech translation is not understanding language itself but connecting it to context. It is entirely possible that, by the time this book goes to print, speech translation systems will be able to reliably find and say an equivalent for most sentences across an array of language combinations. Yet these versions will most likely not take into account the subtle yet vital cues that help human interpreters understand not just what someone is saying but to whom they are saying it, where they are saying it, why they are saying it, how they are saying it and what they are trying to achieve. It's not language that is the problem with speech translation – it's people.

Note

1   "cannot understand what I am talking about."

References

Best, J. 2013, 'IBM Watson: the inside story of how the Jeopardy-winning supercomputer was born, and what it wants to do next', *TechRepublic*. <https://www.techrepublic.com/article/ibm-watson-the-inside-story-of-how-the-jeopardy-winning-supercomputer-was-born-and-what-it-wants-to-do-next/>.

Downie, J. 2015, 'What every client wants? (Re) mapping the trajectory of client expectations research', *Meta: Journal des traducteurs/Meta:Translators' Journal*, vol. 60, no. 1, pp. 18–35.

Dutoit, T. 2013, *An introduction to text-to-speech synthesis*, Springer Science & Business Media.

Fiederer, R. and O'Brien, S. 2009, 'Quality and machine translation: a realistic objective?' *The Journal of Specialised Translation*, vol. 11, pp. 52–74.

Gile, D. 1990, 'L'évaluation de la qualité de l'interprétation par les délégués: une étude de cas', *The Interpreters' Newsletter*, vol. 3, pp. 66–71.

Koehn, P. et al. 2007, 'Moses: open source toolkit for statistical machine translation', in *Proceedings of the 45th annual meeting of the ACL on interactive poster and demonstration sessions*, Association for Computational Linguistics, pp. 177–80.

Koehn, P. 2009, *Statistical machine translation*, Cambridge University Press.

Koehn, P. 2017, 'Neural machine translation', *arXiv Preprint*, viewed 3 January 2019, <http://arxiv.org/abs/1709.07809>.

Läubli, S., Sennrich, R. and Volk, M. 2018, 'Has machine translation achieved human parity? A case for document-level evaluation', *arXiv preprint arXiv:1808.07048*.

Lemetty, S. 1999, *Review of speech synthesis technology*, MTech Thesis. Helsinki University of Technology. <http://research.spa.aalto.fi/publications/theses/lemmet ty_mst/index.html>.

Leprince-Ringuet, D. 2018, 'Why is Google's live translation so bad? We asked some experts', Wired UK, 22 October. <https://www.wired.co.uk/article/live-translation-p ixel-buds>.

Macchi, M. 1998, 'Issues in text-to-speech synthesis', in *Proceedings of IEEE international joint symposia on intelligence and systems, 1998,* IEEE, pp. 318–25.

Och, F. J. 2002, *Statistical machine translation: from single-word models to alignment templates*, PhD Thesis, Bibliothek der RWTH Aachen.

Siemens, G. 2005, 'Connectivism: a learning theory for the digital age', *International Journal of Instructional Technology and Distance Learning Go Top*, vol. 2, no. 1. <http://itdl.org/Journal/Jan_05/article01.htm>.

Sreelekha, S., Bhattacharyya, P. and Malathi, D. 2018, 'Statistical vs. rule-based machine translation: a comparative study on Indian languages', in *International conference on intelligent computing and applications*, Springer, pp. 663–75.

Taylor, C. 2012, *Google Translate turns Obama into Bush, mashable*. <https://mashabl e.com/2012/08/20/google-obama-into-bush/>.

Toral, A. et al. 2018, 'Attaining the unattainable? Reassessing claims of human parity in neural machine translation', *arXiv preprint arXiv:1808.10432*.

Level 2

How machines gained the upper hand

Given the power and potential of human interpreting, we might think that it would seem ridiculous that machines, even with their extraordinary ability to crunch data, would be able to come anywhere close to human performance. The more we investigate interpreting, the more it appears to be a complex, multilayered activity involving not just linguistic skill but social awareness, cultural *nous*, ethical problem solving, and online decision-making. As I write this, it is hard to find any evidence of machines managing any of these. In fact, where one of these skills is required, they have to be programmed in by hand.

Take the case of self-driving cars having to decide whether to preserve the life of one person or many in the event of an unavoidable accident. Rather than have the computer work out its own ethics – a prospect that even the most avid technophile would reject out of hand – philosophers and engineers are having to work together to write ethics into the machine.

The more we investigate interpreting, the fewer binary decisions we find. Interpreting is rarely about intervening or not intervening, being accurate or inaccurate, translating literally or creatively. Instead, as the previous three chapters argued, human interpreters deal most often with inherently fuzzy contexts where every decision is debatable but some decision *has* to be made, with consequences that are rarely fully predictable.

So why do so many people, and some interpreters among them, believe that computers are on the verge of pushing us out of our jobs? Is there even any truth in that claim?

Before we can answer that question, we need to take a step back. To interpret in a way that works in the age of speech translation robots, we have to learn how and why people have come to believe that these robots are going to take over interpreting. Before we can help people see the value that human interpreters bring, we have to understand the messages they are already hearing.

This is why this level is dedicated to understanding the messages people have been hearing about interpreting. The first chapter takes us on a short tour of the public relations messages coming from interpreters themselves by looking at a sample of the ways in which interpreters have talked about their work to the public. While there have been important recent changes, there are long-lasting patterns in the ways interpreters describe their work that will need to be changed if interpreting is to survive in the age of speech translation.

In contrast, providers of speech translation software and devices have a long history of making grandiose promises, few of which have ever come to fruition. It's worth examining the most recent cases to see what interpreters can learn from their success, even if this success has been more in helping people believe a promise than actually delivering on it.

Chapter 4

How we wrecked our own PR

"Translators are self-critical; interpreters are self-confident." I don't quite know who first came up with that, but it is a quote I have heard several times. There is, of course, a grain of truth to it. By its nature, our work involves having the bold-ness to go into an assignment, make quick decisions as to how to deal with dif-ficulties and get on with the job. Rarely, if ever, do you get the chance to go back and do a detailed review of your own work.

But, until very recently, the way that we discussed our work with the public was anything but stridently confident. Instead, a pattern was set whereby inter-preters would concentrate on talking about how much their work was in the back-ground or how much they *didn't* change what was said. The focus was on trying to make interpreters disappear. In fact, even in the upper echelons of the inter-preting world, a guide published by the International Association of Conference Interpreters (AIIC) still advises its members to "make them [the audience] forget they are hearing the speaker through an interpreter" (AIIC, 1999, sec. 3.3). If interpreters are telling each other that, it is worth asking whether the same mes-sage of interpreter invisibility is going out into the wider world.

As with most questions, we can get close to an answer by looking at research. Let's start with the basics. Almost all researchers agree that there was a traditional picture of conference interpreting, which was later superimposed onto other forms of interpreting as they began to professionalise. The professionalisation of confer-ence interpreting and the growth in training institutions became the pattern that other forms of interpreting would seek to copy.

But what was the picture of interpreting that was so influential? In her book *De-/re-contextualizing Conference Interpreting: Interpreters in the Ivory Tower?*, Turkish conference interpreting researcher Ebru Diriker points out that profes-sional associations covering conference interpreting have been remarkably con-sistent in their descriptions of the task. At the time when she wrote the book, AIIC's outward-facing descriptions of interpreting were very close to the position I discussed earlier. As she writes:

> Identification with the original speaker is also presented as a defining feature
> of professional interpreting. "Genuine" interpreters, the AIIC underscores,

"identify closely with the speaker and, while interpreting, [...] adopt the speaker's point of view." Furthermore, according to the AIIC, the finest reward of "genuine" interpreters is to see the audience act "as though the speaker and interpreter were one and the same person."

(Diriker, 2004, p. 33)

Time moves on, and nowadays the AIIC website is as likely to talk about the need for interpreters to have a "well-developed capacity to express themselves in their own language" (AIIC, 2012a) as it is to explain that "interpretation therefore makes use of particular linguistic resources: the original speaker's ideas are transmitted as spoken words, with a particular rhythm and intonation, making use of rhetorical devices and gestures" (AIIC, 2012b). But still, as recently as 2017, the association produced a video encouraging the use of interpreters, titled "Let them hear *you*" (AIIC, 2016; emphasis mine).

Indeed, the overriding message of that video is that working with an interpreter is the best way of ensuring that the "flavours" of *your* language – the humour, style, nuances and the like – are conveyed in the target language *exactly* as they were in the original speech" (emphasis mine). The animation in the video even shows exact copies of the same meal being presented to people from all over the world. Interpreters are so skilled, it seems to suggest, that they can produce clones of your message in another language. To quote the video, "[W]hen an interpreter has been properly prepared, it is as if your carefully crafted dish is being served just as carefully prepared in another language."

The overriding PR message of this video is that interpreters do not make changes. The dish is the same. The flavours are the same. It's just that it has been presented to a different audience. The height of expertise in interpreting is still to make *no difference at all*.

Yet this is far from being a unique message. Around the same time Ebru Diriker's book was released, community interpreting researcher Andrew Clifford pointed to an almost identical ideal being promoted by researchers and professional associations in various forms of community interpreting (Clifford, 2004, pp. 91–92). Ebru Diriker's book also points to analogues of this view appearing in the highly respected work of Danica Seleskovitch (1977; in Diriker, 2004, p. 35). Indeed, she would follow up the book with a paper seven years later pointing out that, despite growing academic research showing that interpreters played an active part of the events at which they worked, little had changed in the way the profession presented itself to the public (Diriker, 2011). It is important to reflect on this PR, which interpreting has built up over generations.

For a good example, it helps to turn one last time to Ebru Diriker's book. She reviewed the impressions of interpreting given in books written by interpreters (2004, pp. 45–48), occasions when interpreters were interviewed by the press (ibid., pp. 42–45), and interviews with interpreters at the event she studied (ibid., pp. 67–73). In all cases, the predominant view was that interpreting involved accurately delivering what the speaker said without additions or omissions, or at least with as few changes as possible.

Recent investigations in conference interpreters' views of their own work have continued to show few changes from those results (see the discussion by Zwischenberger, 2015) and these views are also found very commonly among court interpreters too (Angelelli, 2004b). So foundational has the picture of the invisible interpreter who changes nothing become that researchers often take the time to compare the behaviour of interpreters against this model in some way (for examples, see Roy, 1999; Mason, 2001; Angelelli, 2004a; Angermeyer, 2015). It has also become the foundation for recent theoretical discussions (Zimanyi, 2009; Ozolins, 2016; Downie, 2017).

It is important to understand the commercial and political implications of the picture of great interpreting as being the art of changing nothing or being invisible. As artistic and philosophically lofty as it sounds, it is incredibly difficult to convince people to value something that leaves no trace. "Pay us great rates so we can come to court and make no difference at all" is hardly a useful rallying cry to get better conditions for legal interpreters. "You need interpreters so nothing changes" seems to be a rather confusing message. "Hire a conduit" sounds more like an advertisement for plumbing supplies than a way of helping clients see how powerful interpreting is.

It is not that interpreters or agencies ever deliberately went out to try to make interpreters seem superfluous. It's simply that we looked to build trust with clients and decided that the conduit model, invisibility ideal was the best way to get there.

Actually, in some circumstances, it makes sense. Simultaneous conference interpreting was first thrust in the public eye during the Nuremberg War Trials of 1945–46. While it was born much earlier in a meeting of the International Labour Organisation in Paris, Nuremberg is where interpreting suddenly came to public notice. All those defendants, all those testimonies and the need for the watching world to feel that the trial was just and fair.

In those particular circumstances, the venerable conduit "we don't change anything" model may have seemed very sensible indeed. It would have made for a very uncomfortable trial for lawyers and judges to have to take into account that interpreting always changes the nature of the events in which it appears. The perceived legitimacy of the trials and of the entire legal process would have been in jeopardy.

And later, during the high growth period for international intergovernmental organisations, the power of interpreting was that it enabled international political decision-making without the need for a single diplomatic language. There is powerful symbolism in every country in the world being represented around the same table, with the choice to address the world in your national language. Building the assumption that interpreting does that flawlessly and without any pesky modifications or changes is vital.

There is a powerful argument for saying that interpreting needed the conduit model for the sake of not just *its* legitimacy but for the sake of the legitimacy of the new, multilingual institutions that it enabled. That argument is hard to fault. Yet there are two cracks that run down it.

The first, which we met earlier, is that perfect conduit-model interpreting is a linguistic misnomer. It simply cannot be done. Interpreting always changes something, even by its very presence. Building the reputation of interpreting on the foundation of interpreters being perfect conduits could only last so long. The truth had to come out eventually and it is rarely a good PR day when the world realises that it is impossible to deliver what you promised.

The second, and at this point more important, crack is that the picture of the interpreter who changes nothing includes an ominous hand pointing towards the removal of interpreting altogether. I mentioned in my previous book that it is almost certainly no coincidence that the places where the conduit model has held the most sway are the very same places where interpreting is most under threat. If interpreters change nothing, why bother paying them well? It can't be that hard to do nothing all day. If interpreting means just saying what was said, then let's pull in some untrained bilinguals. They know both languages well enough. If interpreting doesn't involve value judgments, ethical decisions, explanations, cultural awareness, creativity and skill then why not just get computers to do it. It's just about language, right?

That last argument explains why understanding interpreting PR and its spotted history is so vital in the context of discussing the battle between human and machine interpreters. Speech translation, as we have already seen, is built precisely on the conduit model. Its basic principle is simple: say what was said last time, base the output on a predefined, decontextualised corpus, create an algorithm on the basis of written language. All of these approaches assume that interpreting is simply a language production or "sequence to sequence" exercise. No need for human judgment here.

Our battle strategy to survive the coming wave of technological advancement therefore must begin with humbly acknowledging where we have been and how we got to the state we are now in. There is no doubt that the conduit model won interpreting trust and a good reputation, but might it have also have begun to weigh us down?

I entitled this chapter "How we wrecked our own PR" deliberately. There is no sense in which I want to pin the blame on any association or group of interpreters. We are all equally guilty.

Despite the recent growth in attempts to talk about interpreting in more helpful ways, including a very successful TED-Ed video on how interpreters do their work (Magalhaes, 2016) and a viral video on how interpreters do their jobs (Olsen, 2019), a quick browse round most interpreter websites will show a similar picture to the one found in Ebru Diriker's work. If you manage to find an interpreter's website among the jungle of agency and tech websites claiming to offer interpreting, you are very likely to find them talking in vague terms like "accurate and trustworthy," "bridging cultural gaps" or "conveying your message" and lots about their qualifications. That's all very nice, but what you are much less likely to see is anything about the specific differences they have made or the typical outcomes from their work.

The picture gets even clearer if you look at interpreting agencies. There, you might even see them describing interpreters as a "conduit" for what is said by the speaker, alongside lots of non-specific ideas of what interpreters do and, of course, promises to only supply qualified interpreters. Add to this the ever-present promise of round-the-clock availability and the amazing ability to find interpreters no matter the language, no matter the event and it's no wonder that people might start thinking of interpreters as a commodity, to be pulled in at the last moment, who simply relay what was said, with no real thinking required.

Nowadays, there are a good few sites that are beginning to break the rules, but still, if you replaced the text from one website into another, I doubt anyone would notice the difference. If all interpreters are talking exactly the same way about their profession and we are all relying on the same small numbers of attributes to explain why we should be chosen, we are making ourselves interchangeable with each other and eventually, with machines.

None of this is really anyone's fault. Most of us were schooled much more thoroughly in interpreting techniques than marketing techniques, and very few university courses include specific modules in PR. Why should they? Certainly, when I trained as a conference interpreter, the understanding was that most graduates would look to get recruited by some international institution. Those markets were still growing quickly and the private market was seen as a more dangerous route. There was simply no time or point in doing a lot of training in PR skills or marketing in that context.

Interpreting PR hasn't been great because, until recently, it didn't really need to be. Where there were strong private markets for conference interpreting, assignments were gained by word of mouth. Outside of those areas, much of the interpreting that went on was dependent on government contracts, which were determined more by political lobbying than anything else.

The rise of speech translation, coupled with the rise in right-wing, anti-immigrant thinking and isolationist politics has changed the game entirely. The last two are the subject of endless analysis and could easily become a book in themselves. Yet the rise of speech translation is enough in itself to force us to think through the drawbacks of our standard ways of speaking about interpreting. This is all the more pressing given that the makers of speech translation have shown themselves to be far more adept at PR and marketing than interpreters and their associations have ever been. The next chapter will explain their strategies and why they are working so well.

References

AIIC. 1999, 'Practical guide for conference interpreters', *aiic.net*. <http://aiic.net/p/628>.
AIIC. 2012a, *Conference interpreting is the interpretation of a conference*, *aiic.net*. <//aiic.net/page/4003>.

AIIC 2016, *AIIC–Let Them Hear YOU (Eng): The added value of professional interpreters*, *YouTube*. <https://www.youtube.com/watch?v=7E_tQAsep7Y>.

Angelelli, C. 2004a, *Medical interpreting and cross-cultural communication*, Cambridge University Press.

Angelelli, C. 2004b, *Revisiting the interpreter's role: a study of conference, court, and medical interpreters in Canada, Mexico, and the United States*, John Benjamins Publishing Company, Amsterdam.

Angermeyer, P. S. 2015, *Speak English or what?: Codeswitching and Interpreter use in New York city Courts*, Oxford University Press.

Clifford, A. 2004, 'Is fidelity ethical? The social role of the healthcare Interpreter', *TTR: traduction, terminologie, rédaction*, vol. 17, no. 2. <http://www.erudit.org/revue/tt r/2004/v17/n2/013273ar.html>.

Diriker, E. 2004, *De-/re-contextualizing conference interpreting: interpreters in the ivory tower?*, John Benjamins Publishing Company, Amsterdam.

Diriker, E. 2011, 'Agency in conference interpreting: still a Myth?', *Gramma: Journal of Theory and Criticism*, vol. 19, pp. 27–36.

Downie, J. 2017, 'Finding and critiquing the invisible interpreter–a response to Uldis Ozolins', *Interpreting*, vol. 19, no. 2, pp. 260–70.

AIIC. 2012b, 'Interpretation is spoken, translation is written', *aiic.net*. viewed 14 March 2019. <//aiic.net/page/4002>.

Magalhaes, E. 2016, *How interpreters juggle two languages at once*. <https://ed.ted.com/l essons/how-interpreters-juggle-two-languages-at-once-ewandro-magalhaes>.

Mason, I. (ed.) 2001, *Triadic exchanges: studies in dialogue interpreting*, St. Jerome, Manchester.

Olsen, B. 2019, *Watch how interpreters do their jobs | WIRED video | CNE*. viewed 19 July 2019. https://video.wired.com/watch/how-interpreters-do-their-job.

Ozolins, U. 2016, 'The myth of the myth of invisibility?', *Interpreting*, vol. 18, no. 2, pp. 273–84. doi:10.1075/intp.18.2.06ozo.

Roy, C. B. 1999, *Interpreting as a discourse process*, Oxford University Press, New York.

Seleskovitch, D. 1977, 'Why interpreting is not tantamount to translating languages', *The Incorporated Linguist*, vol. 16, no. 2, pp. 27–33.

Zimanyi, K. 2009, 'A diagrammatic approach to redefining the role of the interpreter based on a case study in forensic psychology', *Translation & Interpreting*, vol. 1, no. 2, pp. 55–70.

Zwischenberger, C. 2015, 'Simultaneous conference interpreting and a supernorm that governs it all', *Meta: Journal des traducteurs/Meta:Translators' Journal*, vol. 60, no. 1, pp. 90–111.

Chapter 5

Speech translation's marvellous (but misleading) marketing

If you believe the hype, the interpreting profession is on its last legs. NTT Docomo, the biggest mobile phone network, has at last managed to provide a service that allows anyone with a smartphone to instantly have their words interpreted.

I wrote those words on the Heriot-Watt University LifeinLINCS blog back in 2012. That means that they appeared before Skype rolled out the ability to have your calls "translated in real-time," before Google earbuds and their wonderous ability to let you order pasta in Italian (more on that later) and before Tencent would display the capabilities of their machine conference interpreting technology for all to see.

Speech translation has a history of making a huge marketing and PR splash. In fact, so good have its makers become at their PR that even some interpreters are beginning to believe that they might be a risk to our careers. It's quite likely that you are reading this book either because you yourself fear the upcoming speech translation Armageddon or you are desperately looking for someone to tell you that it won't happen so you can finish your next assignment in peace.

How did we even get here? Those of us who grew up before technology companies gained enough data and finance to tip national elections and affect the destinies of continents will know that for decades, the idea of machines being able to interpret between any two European languages was the stuff of science fiction. From the Babelfish in the *Hitchhiker's Guide to the Galaxy* series by Douglas Adams to Star Trek's Universal Translator, breaking down language barriers seemed to somehow represent the apotheosis of technology, even of human beings themselves. Once you undo the Tower of Babel, you have a species that you can reasonably expect to travel faster than light, end world hunger and create paranoid androids.

Once you undo the Tower of Babel, you have a species that you can reasonably expect to travel faster than light, end world hunger and create paranoid androids.

Leaving aside for the moment the historical fact that language ceased to be a barrier at the precise moment that the first human learned more than one of them, the science fiction trope of the universal translator created a perfect basis for speech translation makers to tout their disruptive solutions. And so it all began.

Historians can have fun trying to chase down the first company to try to sell a machine interpreting solution – as opposed to Machine Translation. What is more important is to note the common threads across the PR and marketing of every single such device. Whether they aim to make it easier and safer for soldiers to communicate with local people or to allow you to chat up a nice French person, all speech translation PR relies on the same basic messages.

Message 1: Linguistic difference is a problem

Talk to anyone who does marketing for a living and they will tell you that you need to start with the problem. And with speech translation, the problem is that it is entirely possible that you might meet someone who speaks a different language to you. Shock! Even worse, that might mean that you can't have a deep, meaningful conversation with them!

In the case of ili, a device promoted in 2016, the real issue raised by the spectre of not being able to speak a language was that you would have no idea how to ask someone for a kiss! How on earth could you harass beautiful people if you didn't have the right language to do it in? In one advert (now not available on their YouTube channel but available here: https://www.youtube.com/watch?v=adWmUe7diJE), a male protagonist announces, "I'm going to try to kiss girls I've never met before, using this translation device, ili."

The underlying message of the advert is that the only thing standing between you and a nice kiss is that pesky language barrier. Bring along the device and you can watch the language barrier fall and get those kisses. Given that a newer advert from the same company uses lots of footage of women's bottoms while they walked with the ili in their back pocket while wearing a range of tight clothing, followed by the claim "ili will change the way you travel," the link between speech translation and sex has simply become only slightly more subliminal.[1]

But of course linguistic difference isn't just a problem because it might stop you winning the hearts of people you are attracted to. It also represents an unnecessary encumbrance on the exploits of the world traveller. We only need to watch an advert by Waverly Labs, creators of the "Pilot Translating Earpiece" – which presumably works outside aircraft cockpits too – to understand that.

Aside from explaining its genesis as the solution to the problem of how to talk to French girls, one of the adverts for the Pilot touts its potential to allow its users to realise the dream of "a life untethered, free of language barriers. It's just that it's no longer a dream any more. It's real."[2] The logic is simple: language barriers are a restriction and only speech translation can set you free. It's nearly messianic.

Google's marketing of their own equivalent: the Pixel Buds with the instant translation function, is much less ground-breaking and more about food than sex.

Instead of changing the way you travel, Google chose to focus the translation section of their marketing blog post on the Pixel Buds on the potential to order food abroad (Google, 2017). The problem here is not that you are a world traveller hoping to make important connections with new people but simply that you really need the waiter in Italy to understand that you want pineapple on your pizza. The language barrier is standing between you and your food, and it needs to be removed!

As obvious as it might seem to state that speech translation is sold on the presumption that linguistic difference is a problem, it bears noting. While anyone who has ever travelled abroad can recognise the horror and fear of trying to find your way around without a scrap of the local language, everyone who has learned a language can explain why linguistic difference can actually be a good thing.

The effort of learning another language brings the rewards not only of learning the French for "World Cup winners" or the German phrase for "losing in the first round" but of understanding an entirely new way of talking about and thinking about the world around us. Languages are inextricably linked to cultures, and learning a language to the point of being able to use it in the real world necessarily means learning the finer points of cultural awareness, protocol and politeness. It's all well and good having a device that can ask for pineapple on your pizza in Italy, but if it doesn't tell you what the likely outcome of such a request might be, it would be better not to have it in the first place!

Calling linguistic difference a "barrier" therefore betrays a deep-seated monolingual, if not monocultural, fear. Being misunderstood or not understood at all is doubtless a problem, but throwing the responsibility to solve that to a machine is even more of a problem. It projects a world where differences in words are the only real barrier in communication. If I could only learn to ask for kisses in Japanese, I could get some, one might think, but that ignores the fact that in some cultures simply making the request in public to someone you have never met is hardly likely to be a successful tactic, no matter how good your device is.

The misleading aspect of all the talk about "the language barrier" is that it is myopically monolingual in its view of linguistic difference and hopelessly naïve about what it would take to solve it. As real as the need to figure out how to ask the way to the bathroom might be if you find yourself in another country, obtaining relief using a smartphone is not the same as "breaking the language barrier" or living "life untethered." In fact, the same problem could have been solved with the help of a tiny, dog-eared phrase book that could be bought for a few pounds from an airport bookshop. It could also be solved by pointing or dancing in just the right way. The difference between phrasebooks and speech translation leads to the next speech translation marketing message.

The misleading aspect of all the talk about "the language barrier" is that it is myopically monolingual in its view of linguistic difference and hopelessly naïve about what it would take to solve it.

Message 2: Solving linguistic problems requires a technical tour de force

If the language barrier is the big scary dragon standing between you and kisses or pizza, then the marketing machine of the speech translation minds are all too ready to present their knights in shining armour: smiling engineers.

Take the founder of ili, who seems more than happy to talk us through the design process and technical superiority of the device – complete with alternating technical drawings and one-way conversations with happy, smiling people.[3] The message is clear: solving the problems of travellers has taken years of development and hard thinking.

As you might expect, the message from Waverly Labs is similar. In the same video that contains the tiny admission that the device was invented due to the allure of talking to a French woman, you can also find a gushing account of the team members involved in the project, from an industrial engineer to someone with a PhD in Machine Translation. Their work is helpfully metaphorically illustrated with footage of happy video calls and even more technical drawings, this time in 3D!

For Google, the importance of engineering is suggested much more subtly. In the blog post I mentioned before, keen eyes will notice that pictures of the ear buds take up much more space than discussions of their capabilities. Search for a marketing or PR blog post on how Google manages speech translation and you will stumble across an article that spends a lot of time on how they manage to teach phones to recognise typed letters, with the claim to have broken the language barrier gracing the final paragraph, right at the end of their technical explanation (Good, 2015).

It's important to note at this point that the claim that technology is needed to break the language barrier is not inaccurate. It is, however, misleading. There is no doubt that it has taken engineers decades to get even close to creating machines or apps that can give a passable rendering of something said in another language. For those interested, there is a rather entertaining series of videos detailing the beginnings of Machine Translation – one of the core technologies underlying speech translation – on the NativLang YouTube channel. Arriving at the current state of language technology has required a number of incredible technical leaps.

Yet that only tells half the story. If you believe the marketing of the machine technology mavens, it is possible to think that humans were trapped into their individual language communities until IT engineers and their friends came along to free us. Just as linguistic difference is framed as a previously insurmountable "language barrier" by speech translation marketing, so the range of possible solutions to communicating with people who speak a different language is reduced beyond recognition.

It simply is not true that the only way to survive abroad is to carry along a tiny device in the back pocket of your tight jeans or an app on your shiny smartphone that connects to your wireless headphones. In the old days, back before companies like Juicero could raise millions by selling the dream of owning a smartphone-operated juicer, preparations for going to another country might involve buying a phrasebook or spending a few hours learning the basics of a language.

True, many people found that despite the best efforts of Berlitz, they still couldn't work out how to ask for directions to the toilet or when the next train for Tokyo was leaving, but the act of sitting down with a tiny book and trying to mouth a few foreign syllables said a lot in itself. It was a handy reminder that you would be the foreigner, and it would be *your* job to make yourself understood. The physical effort of trying to learn a language introduced you to a new culture, a new way of thinking and lots of helpful background information about the place you were visiting.

Swap this for the idea that some friendly, smiling engineers have worked out the problem for you and the picture is very different. Watch the second video from ili closely and you will see that they moved away from mobile apps precisely because they were realising that staring at a smartphone for translation was placing a real barrier between people. Listen to the ad from Waverly Labs and you will hear similar language from them too. Part of the allure of in-ear translation technology is that it seems to remove the problems associated with communicating across language using technology. Yet moving from a smartphone to an earbud simply hides the problem – it doesn't resolve it.

Yes, there is a technical tour de force involved in speech translation, but in trying to make multilingual communication effortless, the ili marketing team manage to promote cultural and linguistic laziness. If you only ever really hear your own language and never have to deal with trying to communicate differently, have you really left your monolingual bubble? If we really want a world without linguistic limits, we need *more* human effort and the skills of human language professionals. Technical achievements will not be enough. In fact, they might just create problems of their own – problems that are far more insidious and potentially dangerous than having to resort to awkward dancing to find the toilet or missing out on kisses.

The problem with seeing technology as the solution to linguistic difference is not that the technology is not impressive but that it creates a fantasy. The fantasy is that all you need to do to be able to communicate with someone from another country is to have some way of using the right words. Few, if any, people with any knowledge of linguistics or intercultural communication would accept that view. The realisation that technology is not sufficient to resolve linguistic and cultural difference leads to the final and much subtler misleading message offered by the promoters of speech translation.

Message 3: Speech translation is perfect

Watch any promotional video on speech translation and you will see a single theme. As soon as people start using the device, their entire world changes and suddenly, miraculously, there is perfect understanding. Anyone who is not familiar with the actual state of Machine Translation and speech translation will be left shocked and amazed by the power of such tiny devices.

In the second ili video, the founder not only shows us footage of people using the device with wonderful results while travelling but he regales us with tales of people who have said that ili completely changed their visit. Watch the video from Waverly Labs and you can see the founder suddenly able to not just talk to a French woman at last but take her round a romantic-looking city, complete with lots of impressive buildings that he seems to know a lot about.

Of course, we should expect little more from adverts. Speech translation devices aren't yet subject to the kinds of advertising scrutiny as medical devices or even food. Since the law does not mandate boringly accurate small print for such products, it is only to be expected that the claims made are general, sweeping and impossibly hard to validate or falsify.

Yet there is no need to browse through the kind of research that was discussed in Chapter 2 to realise that speech translation is far from perfect. Take the following words of wisdom from Nicholas Ruiz, one of the speech translation experts working for Waverly Labs:

> Although Machine Translations may occasionally sound funny, the technology has developed to the point where two conversation partners can understand reasonably well what each one is saying. Machine translation technology can't quite replace high risk translation scenarios where precise translations are critical, but it covers a lot of the need where a professional translation or human interpretation isn't the preferred choice.
>
> (Waverly Labs, 2017)

Notice the key point that "the technology has developed to the point where two conversation partners can understand reasonably well what each one is saying." This is hardly the stuff of joyous discoveries or a new culture or even a pleasant walk round a romantic city with a French woman. It's the stuff of ad hoc "Where is the toilet?," "Is there a Metro station near here?" requests. These are exactly the same use cases, in fact, as phrasebooks. There is no doubt that by the time this book goes to press the technology will have improved, but it will take an awful lot to go from just about squeezing out phrasebooks to changing travelling forever.

The previous sentence in that post is also worth analysing. Here it is:

> In many languages, speech recognition systems are able to recognize over 90% of the words people say, and language pairs like English to Spanish are reaching record highs in accuracy.
>
> (Waverly Labs, 2017)

In this one sentence, which will require a little unpacking, the reality behind the speech translation marketing is revealed, even in the guise of clever PR. The first claim that "speech recognition systems are able to recognize over 90% of the words people say" is telling. As we saw in Chapter 2, Machine Translation, the conceptual core of speech translation, is based on words and only words. It cannot recognise purposes or intention or nuance.

That speech recognition can recognise 90% of the words people speak is impressive. Yet the claim itself shows an understanding of language that is trapped at the level of words. Words are important. This book is made up of words. Yet communication goes far beyond words, and as any interpreter will know, knowing all the right words is not nearly enough for interpreting.

> Knowing all the right words is not nearly enough for interpreting.

Bearing in mind this understanding, the next claim that "language pairs like English to Spanish are reaching record highs in accuracy" becomes far more slippery than it might seem. We have already seen how the definitions of accuracy used in Machine Translation are far from any definitions that would be acceptable to interpreters, and if we are to be unkind, a long way from measuring successful communication. To be fair, however, no one has ever claimed that they were intended for that purpose.

Reaching "record highs for accuracy" therefore is a neat PR phrase that masks deeper issues. Aside from the rather cheeky retort that the impressiveness of reaching a record high really depends on what the previous records were, the point is that accuracy on its own is a failing measure of interpreting quality, especially if it is only measured on the word level. While interpreting researchers are a long way from a robust definition of quality or even of how interpreters interpret, you would still be hard-pressed to find an interpreting researcher who was happy to judge the performance of an interpreter purely on the strength of a side-by-side comparison of transcripts of what was said.

While the marketing hype will always paint speech translation as perfect, reality always barges in fairly quickly. A quick search on YouTube for early reviews on the Pilot Translating Earpiece, for instance, uncovers complaints about functionality and the actual quality delivered. At this point, there is not a single neutral report of anyone using speech translation in the real world for more than a few minutes and not noticing any flaws.

As we saw back in Chapter 3, this is precisely what happened to Tencent when they tried out their Fanyijun system in public. Engineers' reports boasted of excellent levels of accuracy only for it to fail badly when used in the real world. The only fair conclusion is that current ways of measuring the accuracy of speech translation are fatally flawed. Since the systems are currently built precisely to maximise their scores according to these measurements, we have to be critical of any of the claims made by any manufacturer.

So what do we do now?

The reason for this chapter was to help us understand how speech translation companies managed to take advantage of historic failures in interpreting PR and the dreams of science fiction. While it is doubtful that any of the CEOs of these ventures read up on the ways that interpreters presented themselves in public, the decisions taken by interpreters and their associations made life easier for the speech translation people to promote their misleading but superficially convincing messages.

Keen readers will be aware that things are changing in professional interpreting. As I write this chapter, my colleague Judy Jenner has just appeared on an important programme on the US news channel CNN to talk about interpreter confidentiality. As we will see later in the book, interpreters are increasingly learning the importance of being visible to the public while explaining their work clearly, accurately and convincingly.

Yet the challenge of speech translation remains, and the misleading messages promoted by speech translation companies remain current and powerful. How we might begin to counter those messages will be the subject for later chapters. For now, it is enough to begin to understand the arguments used by the peddlers of speech translation and to know their weaknesses.

Faced with the power and capital of these newcomers, it is not at all clear that human interpreters can continue to enjoy the status they have now. Might buyers eventually decide that it is better to pay once for a "good enough" app than to pay each time for human interpreters? In places where professional interpreters are already under pressure, might speech translation be seen as the best solution?

In the next section, it will be up to you to decide. As we move on to that level, it's time for readers to start making their own decisions. Instead of going through the chapters one by one in order, you have the opportunity to choose what you think will be the future of interpreting and see what the future might look like for us and for those who work with us.

Notes

1   The advert can be found here: https://www.youtube.com/watch?v=Rfu7maJjYu4.
2   The advert can be found here: https://www.youtube.com/watch?v=NjjQ5cH_YzI.
3   That video can be found here: https://www.youtube.com/watch?v=nH6LVfQ12A8.

References

Good, O. 2015, 'How Google Translate squeezes deep learning onto a phone', *Google AI Blog*. <http://ai.googleblog.com/2015/07/how-google-translate-squeezes-deep.html>.
Google. 2017, *Google Pixel Buds—wireless headphones that help you do more*, Google. <https://www.blog.google/products/pixel/pixel-buds/>.
Waverly Labs. 2017, 'Interview with Nicholas Ruiz on speech translation', *Waverly Labs*, 14 June. <https://web.archive.org/web/20170915084306; http://www.waverlylabs.co m/2017/06/speech_translation_interview/>.

Level 3

Choose your interpreting future

You have read the background, absorbed different models of interpreting and learned the difference between how humans interpret and how computers attempt to do the same. Now it's time to apply that knowledge and become an interpreting futurist. This level is different from any other. Instead of reading all the chapters in order, you have a choice to make. From now on, you decide what you think the future of interpreting will look like.

If, after all you have read, you think that the days of human interpreting are numbered, go straight to **Chapter 6**. There you will find out what that particular future looks like and what it means for interpreters and humanity.

If you think that legal protection will save human interpreting from the might of the mechanical monsters, go straight to **Chapter 7** to get a taste of that particular future.

If your vision of the future of interpreting sees humans mastering certain limited but presumably financially rewarding niches, your next stop should be **Chapter 8**.

Lastly, if you are ever the optimist and foresee human interpreting becoming the gold standard for multilingual events, hop right on over to **Chapter 9**. At the end of each chapter you will have the opportunity to reconsider your choice and pick another future.

Chapter 6

Human interpreting as a stopgap

Penny pulled on her suit jacket for one last time. This was it: her very last interpreting assignment. The termbank had already sent her the terms, which had been loaded into the app on her tablet that whispered them to her in her sleep. The client's chatbots had slowly explained the purpose of the assignment to her, using words that were more suited to explaining the workings of a bus engine to a six-year-old. And now it was time. With a tinge of sadness, she petted her six cats, plopped their food bowls in front of them, turned off all the lights and headed out the door.

As she headed for the bus – driverless, of course – she couldn't help noticing that she was the only person in her entire street not wearing wireless headphones. If you strained your ear, you could hear snippets of conversation. People had long since been convinced of the benefits of restricting your language to phrases the computers could understand, even when you didn't think they were listening. After a while, you got used to the sound of hundreds of people saying things like "I am going to work. I expect to arrive at 8.45 a.m. GMT" at a measured pace and with no intonation.

Soon, the bus doors opened, as a robotic voice wished her "Good morning, Penny" and a screen nearby displayed her estimated arrival time, having interfaced with her smartphone about her intended route. She sat on the seat that the bus had decided would be optimal, and the bus pulled away from the kerb.

It began to rain. She stared out the window, thinking back to her training. Her parents had warned her about her career prospects. She could still hear her father's deep voice saying "No one needs languages any more, Penny. The computers do all that for us. Why not get a real career? Something in a tech field. I know the plant needs more people to oil the robots. The pay is good and you only need to work six days a month."

She had ignored him. Her tablet was soon full of e-books on notetaking and terminology learning, ethics and technology. The one book her tutors had recommended most was the one she read last and with real trepidation. *Mastering the transition* was all about finding those few areas where clients still wanted humans to interpret. It was the only book not written by an interpreter. Instead, a master programmer from a large software house had taken to writing it as much out of pity than anything else. To this day, she had refused to read the last chapter.

And now here she was, not just in her last chapter as an interpreter but in the last chapter of interpreting as a profession. It was a large conference, with interpreters covering ten languages, including two signed languages. Just this once, the avatars and apps had been given the day off. The title was unforgettable "The Last Human Worker."

Surprisingly, it wasn't actually that difficult. Speaker after speaker stood on the stage, revelling in the achievements of technology. Surgical operations done consistently and efficiently with no need for contact with human doctors and nurses; travel times between major cities halved with no accidents for over a decade; and care for the elderly made so much more sustainable with all-robot provision. There was the odd embarrassing statistic about increases in mental illness due to increased social isolation, but it was waved off with tales of machine learning in psychiatry that could allot the perfect treatment to each sufferer.

The controlled language and the predictability of the talks meant that the conference flew by. Even Penny's usually surly boothmate remarked that it has been the most straightforward assignment of his career.

And then came Jack. Jack was not his real name. No one knew what his real name was. All they knew was that he was off-grid. He walked everywhere or got a lift from friends, as no bus would let him on. He lived in a house with a manual lock and had no social media profiles. To the system, he was nobody. In this room, he had a voice.

Now that he had a voice, he broke the rules. Within the first minute, he had dared to utter phrases that weren't part of the controlled language database everyone had been taught to use. He told entertaining stories, and his jokes were based on unexpected things happening. His ending had everyone on their feet.

> I'm suboptimal. This morning, I took an inefficient route to my mate's house for him to drive me here. I stopped to smell the flowers growing between the cracks in the pavement before the cleaner bots came and yanked them out. I ate a sandwich in his car and got crumbs all over the back seat. I wrote on paper with a pen. Yes, a pen!

> I'm unpredictable. Only God knew when I was going to get up this morning. I mixed three kinds of cereal in my bowl and let the milk spill a bit over the top. I am wearing mismatched socks and I picked my tie at the last minute.

> I'm human. I come up with ideas for useless things that create no economic value. I write books with characters who care and cry and laugh and

don't spend all day checking their social media analytics and readjusting their messaging accordingly. I refuse to let machines tell me how to live my life because I am human and they are not. I create; they process. I imagine; they concatenate. I plan and dream; they schedule and analyse.

It may well be too late, but for the sake of being a real human, dis-connect! Think freely. Coin new words. Break grammar rules. Surprise someone else and yourself with a picture or a song. It doesn't matter if it meets anyone else's criteria. Just have fun. Break the mould. Be you. Be free. Be unpredictable. Be human.

Everyone clapped in perfect rhythm and then filed out to the drinks machines, which scanned their faces and prepared their favourite beverage at just the right temperature to facilitate conversation. Someone had to fetch a cup for Jack, who insisted on boiling his own water with a kettle from his bag and dropping in his own tea bag, getting water on the pristine surface of the table in the process.

Although it was technically against the rules, Penny found him in the corridor and shook his hand enthusiastically.

"I wish I had heard you ten years ago," she said.

"It would probably have been too late, even then," he responded, staring into his cup.

"I know," Penny admitted. "But still, people need to hear your message. Did you video it so I can upload it to social media? It would get thousands of views. "

"I didn't and I hope no one else did," Jack snapped. "If there is one thing I don't need it's another swarm of drones knocking my door and pushing me to sign up to some network."

He paused.

"Anyway, thanks for interpreting this for me. It was nice to work with humans for one last time."

He turned and walked away. Penny grabbed his shoulder as he was leaving.

"Listen, if there is anything I can do. It can't be easy living without tech. I could maybe sneak you some food or something."

Jack smiled.

"Thanks for the offer. Actually, I'm moving outside the city to an old farm someone found. I am hoping I can be self-sufficient. It's about the only way I can hope to say off the grid."

Penny wished him the best and went to gather her coat and bag. As she stood in the cloakroom queue, waiting for her face to be scanned, Jack tried to make his way out of the conference hall with no one seeing. It didn't work. A few meters from the door, two mobile delegate helper robots suddenly blocked his way and two black clad figures seemed to appear out of nowhere.

As Penny was patting her coat to ensure she had everything, she heard Jack say "nope. Not today lads" and watched as he jumped on top of a delegate helper bot, sprung towards the door and ran out. The last she saw him, he was weaving his way down the street, before diving into an alleyway.

Back on the bus, Penny thought back to Jack's words about being human. Life had become so much more predictable. No more misunderstandings. No more getting offended at people using the wrong term. Everything was clear, definite and specific.

With everything so clear, communication and trade had grown almost exponentially, especially with the universal translation and interpreting apps getting to the point where you could almost forget that different languages existed. Connected eye glasses automatically superimposed the translation of signs wherever you were, wireless ear pieces provided the interpreting. It was all so easy.

And yet something was missing. During her training, Penny had heard about some of the great speakers of the past: Martin Luther King, Winston Churchill, Elizabeth I, Maya Angelou. There were no great speakers now. There were lots of people who had lots of information but they had all long since looked for the most efficient way to express their message and the database made them all sound the same anyway. She had looked at images of the great portraits and landscapes of artists in history and then compared them to the AI-abstract art that adorned every bus stop and every museum.

Computers were powerful, and they could do amazing things. Neural networks could find patterns that humans could never have imagined. But in the minutes before her automated sleep inducer lulled her into unconsciousness, Penny wondered whether humans might have lost something in their drive for efficiency and effectiveness. Had technology robbed as much as it had given? She promised herself she would think about it tomorrow.

If the future involves human interpreters being phased out, that change will be symptomatic of much wider societal shifts. As we saw in Chapter 3, one of the biggest challenges for speech translation is the variability of language produced by humans. Controlled language, which is already in use in many technical sectors, would solve that problem. Similarly, the more data that is fed into machine learning algorithms, the better they get at making predictions. It is by no means impossible to imagine a day when our travel plans, spending and even sleep are monitored and rendered more effective by machines.

Inherent in all of these changes is a future where having more data means having more power. Companies who have enough computing power to create algorithms that can interpret what we say flawlessly will likely have enough data on us to also predict our spending, voting patterns and personal habits. In fact, the last three are a lot easier to model than interpreting. To phase out human interpreters is to hand over the power of human interlingual communication to the giants of big data and machine learning. We can only hope that their interests align with those of the people involved in the interpreted event.

A future with fully computerised interpreting, therefore, poses risks not only to interpreters but to their current and future clients. Human interpreters are bound not to take financial advantage of what they discover while interpreting. Any interpreter caught buying or selling shares in a company after interpreting for the managing director would find themselves hauled before a disciplinary committee and the courts. The business model used by the giants of big data is precisely to make some sort of financial gain from the data they gather as they offer free services. It would make no sense for them to offer speech translation without making something back from it. The question is, are clients aware of the potential price?

Underneath the quest for ever-smarter machines is the idea that efficiency is god. An advert that only appears in front of the most suitable audience is far more valuable than one that is sent blindly to the masses. Food produced quickly creates more profit than a meal that has to sit and simmer for hours.

Efficiency is good, but it is not god. Giving an accurate medical diagnosis is an undeniable part of the job of being a family doctor, but the way in which that diagnosis is delivered and the rapport built up with patients is just as important. It takes a certain kind of skill to deliver difficult news and yet still keep the person in the correct mental state to understand their treatment options.

If, as this book has argued, interpreting is as much about people skills as it is about language skills, then even perfectly accurate speech translation will be short of an ingredient. Its success depends almost entirely on communication being reduced to the passing of information. And that in turn depends on human beings adjusting to a world where the emotive and artistic are demoted in favour of the informative and the declarative.

If human interpreters are to be phased out, it will be a move that signals much more than the end of what we now call the "language barrier." The dream of universal communication is inextricably linked to the loss of the unpredictable and the imprecise. It is for all of us to decide whether that is a price worth paying.

This is not the only possible future for interpreting. If you now want to explore a world where human interpreters hang on with legal protection, go to Chapter 7.

If you would like to imagine a world where human interpreters master certain niches where machines cannot work, go to Chapter 8.

If you would like to get to know a future where human interpreting becomes the gold standard for spoken and signed multilingual communication, go to Chapter 9.

Chapter 7

Hanging on with legal help

His name didn't matter, although it was written in dark letters on the torn and bent ID card he flashed at the front security camera as he limped into the building. He plopped his bag down on the security belt, yanked out his tablet and headphones, carefully placed them on a separate tray and wandered up to the body scanner. As the scanner checked him for hidden articles, the security belt pulled in his bag and tablet, ran its own scans and pushed them back out the other side.

"No anomalies. You may proceed, Interpreter #532," squawked a metallic-sounding voice. "Please remove your bag from the belt and be on your way. Good day to you."

He walked along corridors entirely bereft of other humans. He had grown used to the squeak of the lawyers' smart leather shoes as they walked along the corridors or the muted conversations of witnesses chatting with their families or representatives before being called. But now, all of that had gone.

Just before the corridor turned a corner, he stopped. Beside the door of court #7 was a monitor listing the case at which he was supposed to interpret. He scanned the QR code underneath the case name with his tablet, and immediately the case notes appeared on his screen with the names of those involved highlighted and key terms predefined and translated for him. He found an aging leather couch opposite, which creaked unnervingly as he sat down to read the notes. Thirty minutes briefing time and then he would be expected to be in the courtroom.

He was just settling into reading when there was a tap on his shoulder.

"Wha-? Who? Huh?" he stammered, before jolting himself up to a standing position.
"I didn't think anyone else was due here today," he eventually managed to get out.

"Long time, no see. I see you haven't lost any of your eloquence," smiled a rather cheeky-looking Dutch lady, clearly enjoying his discomfort.

"Wow. How long has it been?" he replied, slowly calming down. "What on earth are you doing here?"

"Oh, you know, someone has to mop up the odd case here and there. When there aren't many of us left, the court systems soon run out of people to contact and so, here I am. I'm in Court #9 in about half an hour and I noticed you here." The male interpreter laughed.

"We *are* becoming a rare breed. Still, better a rare breed with protection than an extinct breed in a museum," he said.

"I can't help but think that this isn't what we fought for," the Dutch interpreter said, suddenly serious. "I mean, what have we actually won? The right to be the only profession that still needs to file travel expenses? The badge of being the few people for whom shining shoes still makes sense? A few hours more out of the house each week?"

"Could be worse," the male interpreter shrugged. "We are some of the last professionals left anywhere. At least we have jobs."

The Dutch interpreter was about to reply when a piercing alarm rang out.

"Interpreters #532 and #241, you are engaging in inefficient communication. Please prepare for your upcoming assignments. Failure to perform at accepted levels will result in the suspension of your registration. Final warning."

"Bots, you have to love them," shrugged the Dutch interpreter.

"Because we have no other choice," said the male interpreter before making a show of sitting back in his sofa and placing the tablet in front of his face.

"See you on the other side," he whispered conspiratorially from behind the screen.

About 20 minutes later, there was a muffled bang as the bolts on the courtroom doors slid back and then a whir as a motor pulled the doors open.

"So we're ready then," the male interpreter said to no one in particular as he stood up and wandered in.

Inside, instead of the usual courtroom paraphernalia, there were simply three screens – one on each of the main walls. In the middle of the room stood what looked like a rather fat music stand, with two wires protruding out of it near the top. At the end of one wire was a lapel microphone for the interpreter to wear so that surrounding noise was blocked out. At the end of the other wire were two tiny earbuds, to make sure that the sound from the other participants did not enter the interpreter's microphone.

Interpreter #532 proceeded to follow standard procedures for placing his tablet on the stand and wiring himself up for sound. He took a step back from the stand to check the slack on the wires, turned to the main screen opposite the door where he had come in and nodded twice. He was ready.

Although the witnesses and accused appeared on the screen at various points throughout the case, most of the speaking was delivered by the same voice. It wasn't that it sounded completely wrong, but despite the best efforts of the developers, the Universal Lawyer Bot had never quite managed to adopt natural-sounding intonation and rhythm.

"Mr D G Tal, you stand acc-used of mis-treat-ment of tech-no-log-i-cal ass-ets," it droned, seeming to get slightly stuck on every syllable, as it looked up the sound file for each of them. "Under current pro-to-cols, you will not be asked to file a plea. I will now ex-plain the evi-dence ag-ain-st you."

Interpreter #532 dutifully interpreted everything the bot said, doing his best to avoid the temptation to mock it by adopting the same, halting, clipped delivery. The poor defendant looked entirely bewildered. It can't have been easy, sitting in the booth in the trial room about 50 miles away, with hardly another human in the building. Interpreter #532 could spot the typical behaviours a mile away: the continuously wandering eyes, trying to take everything in, the hesitant responses that were inevitably cut off by the bot as it followed standard trial procedures, the occasional attempt to slip some communication to the interpreter with a look, a gesture, a coy smile.

But he had learned long ago to try his best to ignore them. It was more trouble than it was worth to do anything other than work exactly by the book. His license was due for renewal in a month, and he couldn't afford any demerits. Goodness knows, it was hard enough to survive on the financial allocations he got for having a clean record; being hit with a performance fine would force him to return his license.

The trial ended and the superficially repentant Mr Tal got a brief custodial sentence, which he would spend in a cell with four other humans in a relatively bot-free facility. He wasn't the first person to get himself a few months behind bars, purely for the sake of being in a place where humans cleaned the floors and made the beds and routines were more flexible. Truth be told, Interpreter #532 was tempted to try it himself one day. He knew at least one bot that he would enjoy sab-o-tag-ing.

He left the court on time, heard the doors swing shut and lock behind him, dropped his tablet in his bag, slung it onto his shoulders and headed for the security gate. He dawdled as long as he dared there, hoping that interpreter #241 would make an appearance. He knew better than to wait too long though. The bots treated any unnecessary delays as an attempt to defraud the payment system and that, like most other forms of anomalous behaviour, could lead to a demerit.

To his disappointment, she didn't get back in time. He rescanned his ID card, posed for a quick iris scan and walked through the security door next to the scanner.

"Thank you, Interpreter #532. You may return home on transport pod #500775. This assignment has been added to your monthly allocation and zero demerits have been added to your record. Your work for the court system is appreciated and your license renewal will be processed in accordance with standard operating procedures. You are a credit to the system."

Interpreter #532 couldn't help but let out a cynical laugh as he walked through the wide double doors at the front of the building. From where he now stood, he felt more like a cog in the system than a credit to it. Still, there were worse ways to earn a living.

As I write this chapter, I am returning from the 2018 conference of APTRAD, the Portuguese Association of Translators and Interpreters. Among the topics discussed there was the felt need, among both translators and interpreters, for some kind of legal protection for their work. It's not so much that we can feel in physical danger, although that is still a reality for interpreters in some parts of the world. It's that there seems to be an inherent vulnerability in working in a profession where anyone can call themselves an "interpreter" and try to get work.

> There seems to be an inherent vulnerability in working in a profession where anyone can call themselves an "interpreter" and try to get work.

We have all seen it happen. Aunt Sally or Terry the teenager watches a few YouTube tutorials to learn German or Dutch or Swahili, spends a few months between jobs in the country where that language is spoken and BOOM, here they are as an interpreter, offering their services at an hourly rate that is so low their daily net pay is enough to enjoy a small chocolate bar and a can of something fizzy and non-alcoholic on the way home.

It could be worse though. For every Aunt Sally or Terry the teenager, there is Bob the Invincible. Unlike Sally and Terry, Bob is often relatively well paid and might even know a few choice nuggets about the profession, at least enough to pass as a professional. Unlike Sally and Terry, Bob knows no limits. Sally and Terry might pick off the odd pocket money job here and there, but they will rarely want to take on the high-risk assignments. Their choice isn't altruistic; it just takes too much hard work to get those jobs. Bob, however, is familiar with how much those jobs pay, and Bob *really* likes money.

So Bob dutifully tries to win the contracts for sales meetings or even international conferences. Since he knows quite a bit about rates, he is also smart enough to underbid the true professionals by just enough to look credible and raise a few smiles in the client's procurement office. They are happy to trim 5% of an embarrassingly large budget and Bob is happy enough to pocket a decent amount of cash.

The problem with Bob the Invincible is that his lack of self-knowledge, coupled with his love of cash, can only lead to one possible result. What looks to the client like bargain interpreting turns out to be a heady cocktail of self-assured guesswork, lazy carelessness and blatantly making it all up. Bob looks good and prices well but he delivers nothing but utter rubbish.

Aunt Sally and Terry the teenager mostly just hurt themselves. The clients attracted to their service offering probably didn't care all that much about interpreting anyway. Anyone attracted to their rates without even thinking about what they might be getting is not likely to be in our target market. But Bob attracts the potentially good clients and Bob makes them think that our profession is full of rank amateurs. Bob is a liability.

Faced with a terrible trio like that, regulation seems like the best of all possible worlds, as one of Voltaire's characters might have said. If we could only get the same level of protection as doctors, lawyers, dentists and even plumbers, we could sort this mess out once and for all and Sally, Terry and Bob would be forced out of the market. It sounds wonderful.

Yet despite all the clear advantages to regulation, there are two big problems with it. The nature and scale of these problems might be enough to make us question whether regulation is the panacea we make it out to be.

The first, and most drastic issue is the sheer scale of the task ahead of us in getting legal protection for any part of the profession. In most countries, it is extremely uncommon for new regulated professions to be created. Despite their ubiquity, we still rarely find national regulations on the use of the title "programmer" or "IT consultant" or "social media expert" or even "manager." The vast majority of regulated professions attained this standard hundreds of years ago, when guilds could still restrain supply. Even then, there is an inevitable drift and weakening of the limits. Take a look around at how many people now see themselves as qualified to give out legal advice on GDPR despite never having attended law school (or any real training on Data Protection). How many people claim to be a Herb Doctor or a Weight Loss Doctor or a Parenting Doctor, despite not knowing one end of a stethoscope from another?

As I explain in *Being a Successful Interpreter*, attaining regulation is only possible when there is widespread agreement between buyers, interpreters and interpreting users. If those three stakeholder groups agree, it could be argued that regulation isn't actually necessary. If they can't agree on the standards they would like, regulation is practically impossible.

Governments rarely listen to a single interest group, especially with the complexities of international politics, the requirements of re-election and the busyness or running a country to think about. Regulating a minority profession that most people don't understand is hardly a vote winner.

I am not trying to entirely dismiss the idea of regulation, and I absolutely recognise, and to a certain extent agree with, the impulses behind it. I don't mind interpreters dreaming the impossible dream once in a while, but if we are going to pursue regulatory protection, we need to understand the scale of the task ahead of us and ask whether the attention and resources required would be better spent elsewhere.

> If we are going to pursue regulatory protection, we need to understand the scale of the task ahead of us and ask whether the attention and resources required would be better spent elsewhere.

What would it look like to be a regulated profession? The limited successes that we have seen, such as the first official register of sworn translators and interpreters in Belgium,[1] show us both what it takes and what the results of such regulation might be. In the case of our Belgian colleagues, over 40 years after it began lobbying government and 12 years after its full proposal to the Belgian Justice Minister, they at last achieved a single part of the process – the creation of a national register.

According to the Slator news service, whose coverage of the story first caught my eye, there is a sting in the tale. Alongside the creation of the register, standard translation rates have now been set and those rates are anything but generous. It is no surprise that any government ready to give something to translators and interpreters would look to extract a few concessions for doing so.

The quest for legal regulation is borne out of a need to control who can enter the profession, but it can soon become a route by which we lose control of our work and our rates. Any government that decides to regulate interpreting in any way gains power over our registration requirements and fees, working conditions, rates and even our clients. The route to regulation is a move towards becoming employees, rather than entrepreneurs.

If we find this hard to believe, recent stories from the UK may be enough. Here in the UK, two regulated professions – doctors and criminal defence lawyers – are seeing changes to their payments and conditions that equate to a severe drop in earnings. The money paid via legal aid to lawyers whose defendants don't have the means to pay has been dropping for a long time, and recent cuts and changes to how pay is worked out has simply accelerated the trend. For their part, junior doctors have recently gone on strike due to contract changes that would see a drastic deterioration of their working conditions.

Whoever holds the regulatory strings of a profession soon finds themselves holding the purse strings too. With the prospect of lower budgets hanging over most countries, it is hard to imagine governments deciding to pay interpreters generous rates. Hoping for regulation to save us may not be the best strategy to survive as technology develops.

If our vision of the future of interpreting is that we will hang on with legal help, we may wish to think through the results of our strategy. If our only defence against losing our jobs to machines is handing over the reins of our profession to governments, we might want to think again. I am not at all anti-government or an anarchist, right-winger or small-government thinker. In an ideal world, regulation by a generous, resource-rich government would only have positive effects. I just don't think that we live in that world right now.

Sadly, until taxpayers decide that interpreters are a priority and budgets grow substantially, it would seem that using legal regulation or protection of title as a protective shield against being replaced by machines is an unlikely and unfortunate strategy. Perhaps it's time to imagine a different future for interpreters.

This is not the only possible future for interpreting. If you now want to explore a world where human interpreters are replaced wholesale by machines, go to Chapter 6.

If you would like to imagine a world where human interpreters master certain niches where machines cannot work, go to Chapter 8.

If you would like to get to know a future where human interpreting becomes the gold standard for spoken and signed multilingual communication, go to Chapter 9.

Note

1   https://slator.com/demand-drivers/translators-belgium-achieve-breakthrough-gover
nment-recognition/

Chapter 8

Mastering niches

"Who would really want the job of being a sarcasm translator?"

Her interpreting professor's words rang in Sally's head as she walked to work. Although those words had been first written in a cheeky tweet, she had heard enough of his lectures that her brain automatically played that sentence over and over in her mind. She had laughed off the tweet to begin with and watched joyfully as fellow interpreters jumped in with their reasons why the future was still going to be bright for them. Few interpreters were as enthusiastic now.

She slammed her holdall onto her desk, making sure not to hit the partitions that divided off her space from the interpreters on either side. She unzipped the main section and yanked out her headset, the USB end of the chord chiming off the side of her monitor. The five minutes she would spend untangling it would be a welcome diversion.

With her holdall safely stashed under her desk and her notepad plopped beside her keyboard, she plugged in her headphones to the side of the monitor and logged on. The connection was quick. Her employers had long realised the virtues of taking away the actual computers and replacing them with dumb terminals. They were cheaper, quicker and made sure all the real power was held centrally by the servers. No need for the interpreters to make any decisions as to which applications were open.

For the first assignment, she was simply "on call." Deep in the bowels of the company's basement, the servers cranked out the interpreting of the greetings and early parts of the meeting. Sally's job was mostly just to monitor the machine's output and step in when something arose that was too difficult for it to handle, like humour or, yes, sarcasm.

Every few minutes, she pressed a key to interject, before explaining the issue and offering a version that allowed the principals to carry on. The call finished, she received thanks, hit the button to file the recording to the Process Improvement team and then hit a button to signal that she was available again.

Here came another call and the same routine again. Listen in while the computer handled all of the simple stuff and pitch in occasionally to offer a version of the Chairman's joke that might be funny or to assure everyone that the sales person didn't mean to be offensive, he just didn't understand the culture.

Here came another call and the same routine again. There were some terms that the machines didn't recognise. Sally offered a brief apology and gave the correct version. She assured the principals that the machines would now use her corrections to improve performance and that her employer was very sorry for the inconvenience.

Here came another call. And another. And another. Eventually, her computer flashed up that it was time for her lunch. She yanked out her headphones, threw them into the holdall and wandered down the stairs to eat. Exactly a third of the team were on lunch at the same time and most were already sitting around the flimsy plastic tables their employer provided.

Sally found a seat at a table near some of her friendlier colleagues and pulled out her lunch. Serena and Jo were reminiscing again. There were stories about paid flights and hotels. There were tales about having dinner with clients and hours spent each night manually updating terminology lists.

"You'd never get away with any of that now," said Bob, leaning forwards, with his head resting on his cupped hands. "Who on earth would pay for us to build a term list?"

"Never mind that," chipped in Yelena. "Can you imagine the wasted time spent travelling? Your costs would be sky high to cover that."

Serena leant back on her chair, a smile spreading across her face as the stared at the flawless, white ceiling.

"Oh they were," she beamed. "I remember, when I was still a consultant, that hardly any job came out under four figures and five figures wasn't unusual. Amsterdam one week, Prague the next, with a little jaunt to Paris or Edinburgh to finish the month. The hotels weren't always brilliant, mind you, and you hardly ever got to see the sights but you soon built up enough airmiles to get a little break in the off-season."

She suddenly snapped back into reality as her gaze left the ceiling and met the sullen faces of her colleagues.

"Of course, none of that is possible now. Now we just sit upstairs, under lights controlled by head office, listening to work done by machines, and chipping in to improve a system that we have no control over. What a career."

At that, eating in silence seemed the most appealing option. Even Bob, who was usually good for a joke, didn't feel up to saying much. As Sally stood up to grab a drink from the dispenser, Jo came with her.

"Look, I know it sounds bad but it could be worse," she said. "Serena might well remember the golden days with the flights and hotels but not all of us worked there. For some of us being in a secure job is better than getting paid a pittance and being permanently on call, waiting for administrator to call you to go 15 miles across town for a 30-minute job that you don't even get travel costs for. At least here you know what your wages will be each month."

Sally tried a smile but couldn't really manage it. She did her best at pretending to be comforted.

"Yeah, I can see that," she started. "I can see how stability is attractive."

Jo put a hand on Sally's shoulder.

"Look, I know this isn't what any of us signed up for," she said. "I doubt any university course advertised working eight hours a day in a half cubicle, picking up after the machines. I don't imagine that doing 17 calls a day is what you really wanted to do when you became an interpreter. But we just have to face facts. This is the most environmentally friendly and cash efficient way to do our jobs. It makes life much easier for us and gives the clients the quality they are happy to pay for. It's not perfect, but it's something."

"Oh, it's really something, all right," Sally retorted, turning away and poking the buttons on the drinks dispenser.

"I'm just trying to say," Jo began.

"I know exactly what you are trying to say," Sally interrupted with a shout. "I know what you have been saying since you recruited me to this jumped-up Victorian workhouse. You have been saying it all along. Make the best of things. It's the best we can do. Everyone's happy. I have heard it all before."

She grabbed her drink and stormed off, delivering one final, parting shot.

"I give up, I really do. We are humans, not machines, and I hate, just hate, being treated like some robot's handmaid!"

None of it mattered. None of it ever mattered. The argument ended the same way that it had ended yesterday and the day before and the day before that. The bell sounded for the end of lunch, the team shuffled back to their desks, while another third of the workforce logged out for *their* break.

Serena grabbed a cup of room-temperature water and sat in perfect posture at her place, notepad placed with perfect precision. Bob pinned another pun to the divider on his right, before drawing another stickman comic and thumbtacking it to the divider on his left. Yelena drank half of her coffee, dumped the rest in the sink and dropped the cup in the bin, all before sitting down and getting out her knitting. Jo stopped on the stairs to sigh and made sure to check her quality and call scores on the board before sitting down and getting back to work at exactly the time stated on her time sheet. And Sally? Sally slammed her holdall onto her desk, making sure not to hit the partitions that divided off her space from the interpreters on either side. She unzipped the main section and yanked out her headset, the USB end of the chord chiming off the side of her monitor. The five minutes she would spend untangling it would be a welcome diversion.

And they all went on taking calls and intervening only at those moments when the computers in the basement struggled with something. When their team finished for the day, operations were handed over to another call centre in another country with a different time zone. And on it went, day after day after day, call after call after call, ensuring people could communicate well enough, intervening just enough and being just human enough that the machines still needed them. Day after day after day. Call after call after call.

I have heard it said many times that the survival of interpreters depends on us finding niches where the machines can't go. Maybe that means becoming experts at dealing with sarcasm or ending up as super experts in some fine point of law or business negotiation. Maybe it might mean finding an entire field where, for some reason or another, speech translation is deemed off-menu.

As I write this, I am yet to read proof that this mystical area exists or will exist and no one has yet told me which area it is. Of course, every single interpreter in every setting thinks that it could be theirs. Medical interpreters will tell the world that they are safe as no sane human being would allow machines to make life or death decisions. Well, that's true, with the exception of course of self-driving cars, aeroplane autopilots and automatic fire suppression systems.

My colleagues in diplomatic interpreting maintain that their careers and future are safe. Well, apart from that time when the European Parliament interpreters went on strike due to the imposition of unfair conditions. They got a deal in the end though, which is the main thing.

Court interpreters should have a strong argument for their safety of their jobs. Yes, they should have a strong argument, but in some jurisdictions they are having too hard a time battling against rampant outsourcing, the imposition of unacceptable wages and being replaced by unqualified bilinguals to find the space to make that case.

Conference interpreters on the private market can, in many countries, enjoy good rates and status. They can enjoy such good rates and status that they can momentarily ignore the fact that Tencent, one of the largest technology companies in the world, has already tried to replace them with machines. Thankfully, the results of that particular public experiment sent the company back into the waiting arms of human interpreters, but the fact that they imagined it possible to give conference interpreters a day off should give every conference interpreter cause to think.

Probably those with the wriest smiles should be sign language interpreters. Aside from a few odd-looking signing robotic arms and some clunky student projects, no one has made any headway towards creating machines that can deal with sign language. What matters more to them is the eternal debate about how much of their work will end up in call centres not unlike the one I created for the short story that began this chapter. While the machines don't seem to be creeping up on them, that does not mean that their current working practices are unchangeable.

If this sounds depressing, perhaps it should be. Every form of interpreting in every setting can claim to be the niche that humans should get into to save themselves from the impending robot takeover. Every niche in every setting also has weaknesses where someone with the right (or wrong) sort of mind could make a case for humans being turfed out or exiled to massive contact centres, where they swap independence and the choice of when they have lunch for a stable salary.

The biggest problem with human interpreters trying to find a niche where the machines can't get them is that we can't tell where that niche will be. It might indeed be that there is some mystical field somewhere that speech translation won't touch. It may be that sarcasm, irony and cheek become our greatest weapons in our battle against the bots. We simply don't know.

There is another niche-like argument that is often heard and it is one I have made myself. Many interpreters argue that interpreting involves such subtle cues and such complex interpersonal nuances that computers will always stumble. The logic here is that the very humanity of our clients is itself a niche.

There might be something to that. Even the best neural network for recognising images can be stumped if someone toggles a few pixels to another colour. The odd and culturally determined difference between a happy encouraging smile and the smile given by someone who has just played a trick on you is surely beyond their reach. Could it be that humans are just too unpredictable and, dare I say it, irrational for machines to keep up with us?

Certainly, we could make a case for that possibility. The problem is that not every assignment hinges on subtle cues. Go to your average AGM and no one in the audience is paying much attention to the movement of the finance director's eyebrows as he reads out page after page of figures. The chairman's speech on the future of the water tap industry is hardly going to reach the complexity of a Beckett drama or a Homeric epic.

Some assignments have very little of the subtlety and tough decision-making that would make them candidates for a human-only niche. Yes, the machines might be stumped for now by speakers who get their words wrong, but that might not last too long. Yes, speech translation output might sometimes sound more like Dadaism than serious commercial discourse, but the same was said about Machine Translation and yet we can all see the improvements made there.

If we want a sustainable future for human interpreting, finding niches where machines can't work at all could become an increasingly frustrating habit. There must be a better way, surely.

This is not the only possible future for interpreting. If you now want to explore a world where human interpreters are replaced wholesale by machines, go to Chapter 6.

If you now want to explore a world where human interpreters hang on with legal protection, go to Chapter 7.

If you would like to get to know a future where human interpreting becomes the gold standard for spoken and signed multilingual communication, go to Chapter 9.

Making interpreting matter again

There's no need for fiction in this chapter. Everyone has their favourite interpreting story. You read my all-time favourite back in Chapter 1. I have a favourite story with my favourite boothmate too. My favourite boothmate is a lady by the name of Lora Ward. We trained together at Heriot-Watt University.

> We started working together about two years after graduation. I would rather not tell the story of that particular assignment, as it was a nightmare for me! A couple of years ago, however, the story was very different. Lora had always been a better interpreter than I was, though I have never told her that! Having started getting paid assignments before me, she got a bit more experience under her belt, and she always managed to be a bit smoother in her performance than I could manage.
>
> At one particular assignment, I had an advantage, as I had done a similar one before. It was on the glamourous world of deep-sea fisheries policy. If you have done a meeting on that subject, you will know that those meetings are absolutely full of strange terms, long Latin names and people saying one thing but meaning something subtly different. Oh, and there are often scientists who say the wrong things at the wrong time, too.
>
> The first time you do one of those meetings, you spend your entire first shift looking like a rabbit staring into the headlights of an oncoming truck. The complex terminology, the deliberate choice of phrasing, the references to obscure EU policy documents and to international organisations you have never heard of unless you spend weeks at a time on a longliner: it all combines to create what seems like an impossible situation.
>
> Then you settle down. I still remember seeing Lora at the first break when she realised that, now she had done the first few hours, the rest would just be more of the same. It was hard work, but work that you get used to.
>
> At the start of the assignment, I had seen something that I had never seen before – a slightly worried meeting chair. He approached us, shook our hands and said:
>
> "I've heard you two are Scottish. Is that true?"
>
> "Aye," we said, practically in unison.
>
> The sweat visibly dried up on his forehead.

"I'm very glad to hear that. We have fishermen from Peterhead here today. I might listen into the French to see if I get on better with that. Oh, and can you do northern French?"

We both laughed. That was home turf for both of us.

Over two days, we helped iron out details of policy recommendations to be sent to the European Commission, we enabled environmentalists and fishermen to come to an agreement on the size and kind of gear to be used in various parts of the sea and we even opened the way for a discussion as to the accuracy of remotely gathered boat movement data. It was all pretty highbrow stuff, and within a few hours it felt like we were becoming mini-experts on the topic. Although, to be sure, we still kept our term lists close at hand at all times.

Over those same two days, we helped save a species from extinction, learned the finer points of the habits of a single-celled organism and allowed one fisherman to express his incredibly emotional and emotive views on fishing rights on a patch of sea that his father fished and his father before him and his father before that. The high point would come at some point on the second day when yet another patch of sea was being discussed. No, I can't remember which one and couldn't tell you even if I did.

There was some discussion of how to get policy right for some patch of sea that was rich in catch but had real natural importance for the health of the sea around it. One French fisherman, in an attempt to proffer a compromise, said that maybe fishermen could still fish there but it would become "une zone étroitement contrôlée." To this day, I don't know if he coined that particular term or if it was established in some law somewhere that I had never read.

Apart from the initial "une" (one/a), there are at least three ways of translating each of the remaining words into English. Context helped a bit, but all that did was tell us that he wasn't talking about a security cordon in an airport.

If I had been translating that term for the meeting minutes or for some policy document, I would have had time to search laws and procedures, consult corpora, check collocation dictionaries. But I wasn't translating, I was interpreting simultaneously, with a fairly short lag time.

I came up with something like "closely monitored area" and passed Lora the mic as the speaker changed. To our sheer horror, the next speaker was the chair who asked entirely innocently:

"Would it be useful to discuss exactly what was meant by a closely monitored area? Could you maybe clarify what you meant by that?"

I will never forget how fast I scribbled down the original French term and my quickly thought out English version for Lora who gave me the look that tells you that you definitely *cannot* leave the booth in the next thirty minutes!

For the next shift and a bit, the meeting discussed exactly what was meant by that term before deciding to include it in the policy recommendation. It's not really a claim to fame – more of an admission of guilt on my part.

At the end of the meeting, after making our small contribution to the survival of Scottish fish and the livelihoods of Scottish and French fishermen, we got ready to leave. The same chair who had greeted us with mild panic now bade us goodbye with a wide smile.

"Excellent work. We couldn't have done it without you."

And this time, we believed him.

Every interpreter has a story like that one. Every interpreter can tell stories of deals being done, lives being saved, justice being delivered, experts learning more. In addition to the story I just told, I could tell the story of an audience amazed at the skill of my Italian colleagues who interpreted a technical and emotional speech on cleaning up after a fatal accident or the incredible work of my colleague who regularly interprets at Rugby press conferences. We all have stories. We all know the power of interpreting. We all have some clients who know that too.

It is possible for clients to see human interpreting not as some annoying cost item that has to be ticked off but as a vital part of their work that adds far more to their business or organisation than it costs. In fact, when I did my PhD, I found one organisation that sees things that way. In one church in Germany, interpreting is deemed so important that it is written into the constitution. Even the top leaders said that they learned from interpreters and took on board their concerns or suggestions. Two senior leaders even went so far as saying that the organisation could not achieve its goals without interpreters.

It sounds too good to be true. Could it be possible that anything more than a tiny majority of organisations and clients would finally get it? Surely, we can't expect every interpreting buyer to be converted into superfans.

The truth is that, like every other future of interpreting, this one comes with its own costs. The cost of mass adoption of speech translation was the impoverishment of human communication and the slide into predictability and controlled language. The price of legal protection was surrendering control. Occupying niches came with the danger of being restricted to a small set of domains and subjects that may or may not provide viable futures. The cost of being the gold standard is taking interpreting seriously.

Taking interpreting seriously. It doesn't seem like much of a cost, does it? Surely all professional interpreters do that? Sadly, we all know exceptions. When I say that the cost of human interpreting being seen as the gold standard is taking interpreting seriously, I don't just mean the need for Continued Professional Development, PR and marketing or the need to keep up with what researchers are discovering. Taking interpreting seriously means abandoning once and for all any thoughts of being able to turn up at a job, do our stuff and then go home, with our only connection with clients being a cursory email to send invoices.

Taking interpreting seriously means taking a keen interest not just in the niceties of terminology research or vocal care, it means being awake enough to understand why interpreting is taking place and how best to deliver it at that event for that client. It might mean admitting that some forms of interpreting are better delivered by staffers, even though we might wish to keep our freelance status.

Let me explain exactly what I mean by "taking interpreting seriously" with an example. Imagine that you have been asked to advise a speaker who will be speaking to a monolingual audience who just happen to speak a different language than the speaker. Maybe the speaker speaks Klingon and the audience speak Romulan. While this isn't your combination, you have been asked to give advice on how best to set up interpreting.

Some trained interpreters, knowing that many interpreters prefer to work in the simultaneous mode would simply send over a price for two Klingon to Romulan conference interpreters and the requisite interpreting kit. Others might start asking questions about the length of the speech and think about hiring a single consecutive interpreter instead. Perhaps some tech-savvy interpreters would contemplate whether the entire thing could be done remotely.

In their decision-making, each of these groups is seeing interpreting in a certain way. For them, it is a service with a certain set of expected practices and some more preferences. Their job is then to convince the client to buy the kind of interpreting they want to sell. It could be that they revert to the standard operating procedures and contract from the association they are part of or maybe they just decide that they like a particular supplier and want to use them.

All of these cases have the interpreter at the centre of decision-making. The key question is "What is best for the interpreters?" None of this reasoning is wrong. There are good reasons for adhering to accepted standards and going back to suppliers we know and trust. But perhaps putting interpreters at the centre is an issue.

Within the incredible, inspiring, amazing organisation I studied for my PhD, where interpreting was seen as integral and leaders always listened, it was somewhat surprising to note that the purpose of interpreting was as important as the interpreting itself. Their chief interpreter at the time made it very clear that interpreting was important because of what it enabled the organisation to do – reach and teach people who would be otherwise out of reach. The purpose of the interpreting drove the decisions made about interpreters. Organisational vision drove interpreting practice.

Taking interpreting seriously means understanding that the purpose of the interpreting at a particular event or appointment or meeting should always drive our interpreting decisions. Standards and accepted best practices are absolutely vital, but which standards to apply should be determined by the needs of the situation and the goals of the organisation.

The poor Klingon speaker who needs interpreting into Romulan doesn't need an instant quote. He or she needs someone who actually cares about why he or she is speaking, the audience he or she is speaking to and the purposes of the talk. If the speech is some kind of motivational talk, where audience reactions and a sense of connection are important, long consecutive with notes is not likely to be that useful. Instead, some kind of on-stage short consecutive might be the best way to encourage audience participation since the interpreter on stage could work as an initial audience (check out Vigouroux, 2010 for a nice example of this at work). Simultaneous interpreting might also work, but perhaps here the reactions and visible presence of the interpreter could be an important part of the performance.

If, on the other hand, the speaker is delivering some kind of after dinner speech, perhaps long consecutive could be best. It has a long history of being used on such occasions and hardly anyone would relish the prospect of wrestling with bulky IR receivers while trying to remove parsley from between their teeth.

The context could instead be some kind of interplanetary academic conference with our Klingon speaker delivering the perfect keynote, with accompanying slides. In this case, it would make sense to deliver the whole thing with the help of simultaneous interpreting.

That is a rather silly example, especially for any Star Trek fans reading this, but the basic principle is the same. The price of human interpreting being the gold standard is likely to be the move of interpreters from being service providers, who seek adherence to their preferences at all costs, to being experts who give advice and recommendations based on their knowledge of interpreting and commitment to getting clients the best results possible. In the future, every interpreter will need to be a consultant interpreter.

I can hear the cries of dismay and disagreement already. I am sure many readers are desperate to point out that not every doctor is a consultant and not every IT technician is a systems analyst. That is true. Every profession needs both the high-flying experts and the everyday workers. Yet in many professions, everyone does have their own expertise to add. Every doctor is some kind of specialist who in turn knows other specialists to refer people to when needed. Each lawyer knows their little corner well and understands when and how to refer people to other specialists.

The application of this to interpreting is that each interpreter will have to know their particular part of interpreting extremely well and understand how to apply their knowledge to help clients get the best results. You might be a staff sign language interpreter for the police with specific knowledge in how to negotiate cultural difference in witness interviews. You should be looking to develop that knowledge and become the person that the police come to for advice in how to get the best from interpreters in witness interviews. However, if they come to you looking for advice on how best to deploy interpreters across their organisation or how to manage a crime prevention conference, you would need to pass them onto the experts in the organisational implementation of interpreting and a consultant conference interpreter, respectively.

Taking interpreting seriously means building up specific knowledge that can be used to create better interpreting – not interpreting that makes interpreters more comfortable but interpreting that produces the best results, however those results might be measured.

It has to be said that, while the preferences of interpreters are not at the core of taking interpreting seriously, interpreter well-being and knowing what makes for better interpreter performance will be. All good standards are there for a reason, after all. An important part of every interpreter's expertise will be understanding what makes for successful interpreting and what makes the poor interpreter fall apart. No one would seriously suggest that we should adopt unhealthy working practices for the sake of winning a client. Cramped, overworked interpreters will never produce good work. Yet it might just be that our preferred mode or hiring practice or room layout might not be the best one for the particular event or appointment at which we are interpreting. In such cases, it is a no-brainer to ditch our own thinking in return for making sure that the event is a success.

The big problem with making interpreting matter is that it will take interpreters who care. Those interpreters who we hear griping about the temperature of the water or staring at their watches all day will simply not have a job. Clients can spot that nonsense a mile away. Grumpy delivery will never be a gold standard, nor will apathetic yawning or treating each assignment as nothing more than a rather long-winded way to earn a crust. If human interpreting is to matter to our clients, its results need to matter to us.

Reference

Vigouroux, C. B. 2010, 'Double-mouthed discourse: interpreting, framing, and participant roles', *Journal of Sociolinguistics*, vol. 14, no. 3, pp. 341–69.

Level 4

Interpreting that beats the bots

We have seen four possible visions of the future of interpreting, and I might just have given away which I think is best. Now we are left with the tricky question of how to get there. At this point, we have to leave scientific research behind and rely on good old personal experience and a bit of imagination. By definition, we cannot do experiments or observations of the future. We can, however, look at patterns in the present and project them forwards to imagine where they are likely to lead.

This section deals with four strategies that are going to be vital for the future of interpreting. All four of them involve evolutionary, or in some cases revolutionary, changes. It is no surprise that all of them, without exception, are built upon the foundational ideas covered in **Level 1**. Just like in a good computer game, the skills you learn right at the start will prove to be exactly the ones you need to finish.

With the understanding that the very presence of an interpreter in a situation changes it irrevocably and bearing in mind the argument that it is far more useful to be open about the difference interpreting makes than to try to gain a reputation on the basis of making no difference at all, we can now proceed to the strategies that look the most promising for the future of our profession. There is no better place to start building the future than where we started examining our present: just what do people think interpreting is and how can we change that?

Chapter 10

Beating the bots Stage One: taking back interpreting PR

We have seen various versions of the future of interpreting and we have looked closely at how the promoters and developers of speech translation have set about positioning their products as the realisation of the dream of flawless, effortless interlingual communication. Now we face the uncomfortable fact that interpreters cannot control the future of their profession on their own. It is not sufficient simply for interpreters to believe that their work is valuable and better suited to high-value events than speech translation – we must convince the public and potential clients of that.

> It is not sufficient simply for interpreters to believe that their work is valuable and better suited to high-value events than speech translation – we must convince the public and potential clients of that.

This is where this chapter comes in. Whereas the next chapter will concentrate entirely on how we market interpreting, to move clients closer to wanting to buy it, this chapter concentrates on interpreting PR (public relations): how we convince the public and potential clients that interpreting is worthwhile.

The difference between PR and marketing and the essential nature of both has been a major point of confusion whenever I discuss them. Some interpreters argue that PR is pointless, as even the best PR will never win us clients. Why invest time and money and thought in an activity which, at best, makes people feel all warm and fuzzy about interpreting but generates no income? Other interpreters find it difficult to separate the two activities and try to argue that marketing and PR are essentially the same thing.

My response is always to show the chart below, illustrating the sales process of interpreting, from becoming generally aware that interpreting exists and is a good thing to finally choosing a specific interpreter.

Stage	Message	Outcome
PR (public relations)	Interpreting makes a positive difference	The public, press and politicians are more supportive of interpreting and appreciate its place in society and business
Client Education	Here's how to ensure it makes more of a difference	Potential buyers make better decisions as to when to use interpreting and how to hire interpreters
Marketing	Here's how it can make more of a difference in a company in your sector	Potential buyers in specific sectors (manufacturing, law, events, etc.) read, understand and are attracted by case studies of the power of interpreting
Sales	Here's how I can deliver that difference to you	Buyers are motivated to choose a specific interpreting supplier and that supplier (and the interpreters they work with) wins the sale to deliver interpreting at a specific event

The point of this table is that people will tend to need to go through each of the stages in turn before they are ready to buy. It is unlikely that someone will spend several thousand pounds on interpreting from a specific provider if they aren't clear that interpreting is valuable. Similarly, many interpreters will have had the frustration of trying to convince clients to adopt best practices when they have the strange impression that interpreters can work well with the equivalent of a tin can and a piece of string.

If we really want clients to believe that human interpreting is the best solution for events that really matter, we have to take the time to convince them that interpreting is actually a valuable activity. And that is where PR comes in.

PR In practice

Let's take a simple example. In early June 2018, Lord Burnett of Malden, the Lord Chief Justice of England and Wales predicted that court interpreters would be replaced by machines "within a few years." That claim is not at all rare. The question is: how should the profession respond?

Within a day of the report containing that claim being released in *The Law Society Gazette*, a team from the Institute of Translation and Interpreting (ITI), the leading professional association in the United Kingdom for the translation and interpreting sector, put together an open letter and a press release carefully rebutting Lord Burnett's claim. Better yet, the letter also mentioned the importance of court interpreting in the justice sector and linked poor interpreting standards and the use of speech translation with miscarriages of justice.

Traditionally, interpreters, if they responded at all, would go on and on about how wonderful human interpreters are and how machines could get nowhere near. Traditionally, such responses would miss the mark. To make a difference and to earn equal coverage in the press as the original claim from the Lord Chief Justice, the team from ITI had to show the value of interpreting to the judicial process and show clear evidence as to why this same value could not be provided by machines. In short, to generate good PR for interpreting, they had to move away from general claims that interpreters are brilliant and move towards expressing the value of interpreting in terms that make sense for a given audience. PR is always targeted, even if the message is quite general.

What is particularly interesting about the ITI response is not so much that it gained coverage in many of the same outlets that covered the original story but that it subsequently went on to generate its own independent press coverage. Within a month of its appearance, a legal publication aimed at barristers approached the Institute for a brand new article on interpreters in the legal system and whether machines could do their work. At the time of writing, it is too early to start evaluating any long-term difference, but awareness raising is important in itself, especially when court interpreting is so often seen as almost a cost item by governments.

For human interpreting to be seen as the gold standard, associations and individual interpreters will need to work together to continually generate excellent PR. If we want our rates to increase or our conditions to improve or our ability to create value to grow, the first step will have to be to give our work a PR makeover.

Learning from another sector

Interpreting isn't alone as a profession that desperately needs a PR makeover. Ironically, the events industry, a key sector for conference and business interpreters, has had its own trials. Just as most interpreters have met a client with a mythical "Uncle Bob," who can apparently deliver broadcast-quality French or Dutch or Chinese interpreting for a fraction of the price of any "professional" interpreter, so the events industry has had to struggle with clients thinking that they could do everything themselves. What's more, given the eternal battle with budgets and the need for sector-friendly government regulation, event management companies and their suppliers – such as hotels, entertainment agencies, travel agents and so on – soon realised that good PR could open up opportunities that would have been otherwise out of reach.

As I found when I visited the EventIt show in Glasgow in 2018, improvements in events industry PR came about when companies in the sector learned how to speak and write in ways that excited their audience. One of the speakers was Alistair Turner of Eight PR, whom I interviewed for this chapter. His opinions helped me see just how simple and yet profound changes in PR can be.

His first insight was that PR is essentially reputation management. He pointed out that the UK PR Consultants Association have boiled down its essence to being "the result of what you do, what you say and what others say about you."

As an interpreter, I realised very quickly that, while we are all ready to run around burnishing our own reputations, we don't always take the time to realise that we are responsible for the reputation of interpreting as a profession too. Most of us will have met clients who only have bad things to say about interpreters. This interpreter kept turning up late or these interpreters didn't take the time to learn the requisite terminology or these other interpreters have obvious attitude issues and are difficult to work with.

Before we get on with telling the whole world how brilliant we are, we need to look in the mirror and ensure that the way we interact with the people we meet at work will be a good representation of our profession. We can cling all we like to ISO standards and agreed terms, and those are important, but if all clients associate us with our quibbles over the temperature of the water in the booth or the comfort of the seat in the doctor's surgery, we really need to get over ourselves!

As my friend, colleague and co-host of the Troublesome Terps podcast, Alexander Gansmeier, is fond of saying, "Interpreters should not be divas." If we build a reputation of being hard to please and hard to work with, we are handing over the future to the machines.

To return to Alistair's words, "PR is reputation management." He pointed out that the best way to build that reputation is to be doing good things. He emphasised that this doesn't just mean making good products but making good decisions, looking out for the communities around us and building interest groups for whom our work matters.

This, to me, means a complete about-turn from our usual ways of thinking and talking about interpreting. We have grown used to talking about interpreting as a complicated linguistic skill or as an important facet of maintaining human rights. It is both those things. As important as those facts are, however, they don't win over the public and potential clients. What matters to other people is what matters to other people. That might be a tautology, but it's also true. If interpreting is going to have better PR, we need to discover and promote the value that it has for people who right now might not even be able to tell the difference between an interpreter and a translator.

A good way to summarise that point is that, for Alistair, "[G]ood PR is about talking about the wider issues that affect you and your customers." For us interpreters, that will inevitably mean actually caring about the issues affecting our customers too. Are political shifts making them look further afield for new places to sell? Is regulation forcing them to get interpreting when they might not have bothered before? Is there a new technology that is changing their workflows?

There is one key ingredient left in all of this. It's all well and good to try to manage a reputation and speak about the things that concern clients, but we still need an actual message. Alistair's recounted two important lessons from the history of events industry PR that are instructive for our own efforts. His first, and most important lesson is that, in his words, it is a "cardinal sin" to talk about what you do rather than the difference you make to clients. Over the past ten years, the events industry has moved from talking about events to talking about "experiences" and from talking about "moments" to talking about "memories." Those might sound like minor changes or even like buzzwords, but they represented a shift in the way the events industry positioned itself.

By understanding what clients wanted from events and the words they use when they have had a really good event, the industry was able to learn to speak to potential clients in terms they find meaningful. For Alistair, this shift was all about relevance – ensuring that the messages targeted at clients were relevant to them.

Interpreting has historically not been great at that, as we saw in Chapter 4. Perhaps the most important takeaway from this chapter is that we are now at a critical time when we need to work hard at listening to clients so we can master our own messaging. Aside from fulfilling legal requirements, what does a hospital get out of hiring skilled professional interpreters instead of relying on hospital cleaners or bilingual nurses? What positive difference does using expert court interpreters bring to the justice system? If a company is considering hiring an interpreter for their next sales meeting, what tangible outcomes can they expect?

For too long, we have been in protest mode, standing strong to defend our little bit of territory and blow raspberries at anyone who dares to question our orthodoxy, especially if they happen to be interpreting buyers. I have no doubt at all that protest is sometimes necessary and we have much to protest about, but how much has that really won us?

If protest mode was all we needed, court interpreting in the UK would be the picture of good practice, military interpreters would be given automatic right of residence and any talk of subpoenaing presidential interpreters would disappear like a puff of smoke. Protest mode is powerful, but getting the right messaging does much more. It opens doors to opportunities to explain to clients how they benefit from best practice (and if they don't benefit, it's probably not best practice). Good messaging also raises awareness of the power of what we do and brings others onside. Who would you give more to: the person twisting your arm to try to force you to do something or the person who won your trust and your admiration?

For messaging to work, it needs everyone to get on board. Alistair described in detail how the events industry had to get key associations to subscribe to the need for better messaging and then produce coherent messaging between them. As the associations got on board, individual businesses did too. While some large companies with deep pockets weren't exactly early adopters and were happy to do their own merry thing, eventually the momentum caught up with them and they got on board too.

That is a good road map for interpreting too. There are key associations around the world that have the power to set the agenda and direct the messaging. Even if only a few of them jumped into consistently telling people about the power and potential of interpreting, with stories and examples, that would be a good start. It would be even better if they could organise a coordinated campaign.

The majority of the people reading this are not association leaders. Yet that makes them no less important. While it might be tempting to sit back and wait for an association to create great messaging, every single interpreter has a responsibility to think through the PR consequences of their actions too. In many cities, interpreters aren't common, so a single interpreter can easily be the only picture that people see of the profession. To put it bluntly, if we act cantankerous, stuffy and inflexible, then people will naturally see interpreting that way and work harder to get rid of us. If we can show by our actions that we actually care about the worlds our clients live in and how to make interpreting work for them, the siren's song of speech translation might seem a little bit less attractive.

Think about it this way: the speech translation mavens have spent millions of dollars and years of their time creating the impression that they are the great technological heroes ready to rid the world of miscommunication by making interlingual communication as effortless as ordering a pizza. For them, the ideal world is one where you don't need human interpreters anymore. Yet we know that, for many businesses and organisations, the ideal world is one where they get to work with human interpreters. Imagine a world where doctors look forward to interpreted consultations, as they go much better than monolingual ones. Imagine businesses positively wanting to hire human interpreters, as they deliver value that they simply can't find anywhere else.

How do we get people to listen? For the events industry, the first step was to use key influencers to influence the sector itself, helping everyone to learn to see the benefits of agreeing on a clear consistent message. From there, the message could go out, again using influencers, to affect the wider world of government and buyers.

This process of taking messages out actually began with looking at the people and organisations that were already convinced of the value of the events sector and understanding what they were saying. By working with companies that already saw the benefit of the sector, the events industry could gain traction more easily. On this point, however, interpreting needs to make a sector-changing decision.

The biggest PR decision our sector must take

Like almost every interpreter I know, I was inculcated with certain basic interpreting values during my training: don't embellish on what the speaker said, don't take sides and, of course, never, ever breach professional confidentiality. For many interpreters, the last duty tends to sound like "never tell anyone anything about what you are doing. Certainly, never tell anyone who you are working for."

Does that sound familiar? Knowing the importance of helping people see the value of interpreting, I was challenged by the fact that Alistair was firm that the events sector had needed to encourage clients to go out and tell the world their story of what events meant for them. Events companies themselves had also moved towards working with clients to tell the story of the impact of individual events.

Let's think about this for a moment: an entire industry improved its PR by talking about specific events and how they had made a difference to specific, named clients. That made me nervous. I know all about the standards of interpreting and our views on client trust. I asked Alistair if the same outcomes could arise from using anonymised stories. This was his response.

> Confidentiality and PR is a constant battle. Give people an incentive to share their story and then it is less of a problem for them. Stories need to play into authenticity. You have to ask people permission and convince them to share. Have the hard conversation with clients beforehand. Even the big companies will care about doing great business. They can get credit for the big event.

Perhaps it's time to rethink interpreting PR. Of course, there are occasions where it will never be right or even legal to share. No one needs to know about interpreting Mr Bloggs' visit to the urologist or Mrs Smith's consultation with her divorce lawyer. Where interpreting is covered by legal restrictions or where people's privacy is at stake, we don't even need to ask if we can share. We know we can't.

Yet there are plenty of events where interpreting takes place in public areas: live-streamed conferences, international press events, award dinners, TV shows, even business negotiations that later lead to publicly announced deals. In those cases, it might make sense to suggest to clients that, if they are going to be talking about the success of the event or the importance of the deal anyway, they might like to slip in a few lines about the difference the interpreters made. If a client is going to go public with the amazing results they got, it might be worthwhile asking if the interpreter could publish it, minus any commercially sensitive details, as a case study. It's free publicity for them, some nice marketing for the interpreter and good sector PR too.

There are stories of the power of interpreting that are waiting to be told, stories that need to be told if we are ever to make it to a world where interpreters are valued and where human interpreting is seen as the gold standard. Before we go on to the next step in the process, let's briefly recap what I learned in my interview with Alistair Turner and what that means for interpreting.

A sketch of the future of interpreting PR

Recently, a colleague by the name of Hugo Menendez started a daring campaign to help interpreters appreciate the importance of not breaching client confidentiality on social media. He called it "#1ntHUSH." In this chapter, it has become clear that, while the #1ntHUSH campaign is absolutely needed, we probably need a converse campaign too – let's call it "#1ntSHOUT" or maybe "#visible1nt."

What should this campaign look like? If human interpreting is to move from being a necessary but begrudged cost that buyers are desperate to replace with machines to being a valuable service that has obvious benefits for everyone who uses it, we need to start by agreeing on the key messages that we want the public, buyers, users and governments to understand. Some of these messages might be familiar; some might be uncomfortably new.

We could start by reducing our reliance in protesting and building the case that interpreting actually improves every area of society it touches. Excellent court interpreting makes justice fairer, more accessible and less prone to error. In doing so, it reduces costs and keeps the system oiled.

Interpreting in medicine saves lives, allows staff to use their time more effectively, reduces errors and can even *reduce* expenses by getting patients access to the care they need more quickly.

Interpreting in business enables businesses to do deals that would be otherwise impossible, builds reputations across borders and cultures, and allows the sharing of information and expertise. Business leaders have argued for the importance of diversity for decades. Interpreting enables it to an extent rarely seen.

We could do the same for every single area of society where we find professional interpreters. Perhaps the single central message for interpreting is that it changes lives. Perhaps it might do us some good to step away from our fixation with being invisible so we can swap it for the stories of the difference we make.

Stories are indeed an integral part of the future of interpreting PR. As uncomfortable as it sounds, we need to start working with clients to look for places where they want to tell the story of what interpreting did for them. We might also need to be a bit braver and ask them if we can write case studies about the successes they are getting because of interpreting.

Even in cases where we can't or shouldn't name the people involved or go into detail, we do need to find ways of working with clients to talk in general terms about the benefits of human interpreting. Quite simply, if we don't, we are handing over our futures to those who can tell convincing stories, even if those stories aren't perfectly accurate.

We can't do any of this on our own. We need to seek out influencers who will talk up the value of interpreting. We need to partner with clients. Mostly what we need to do is work together. Professional associations need to put aside differences and carve out budgets, large buyers need to be persuaded and individual interpreters need to remember that they are interpreting ambassadors. It won't be easy, but the alternative is much worse.

Chapter 11

Marketing interpreting that matters

It's all well and good if people are thinking nice things about interpreting. Most interpreters would agree that we could do with some good publicity. The problem with PR is that, no matter how good it gets, it won't put extra cash in our pockets or win us more clients. At least, it can't do it directly. If we want new clients or new markets, we need to go a step further, we need marketing.

From the last chapter, the differences between PR and marketing should be clear. PR is about showing people that interpreting makes a positive difference. It leads politicians, press and the public to be more supportive of interpreting. Marketing is more specific. Marketing shows one specific audience how it can make a difference in their sector and their lives. Get marketing right and we shape the decisions of individual potential buyers as to how they buy interpreting and who they buy it from. Before we can look more closely at that process, it's important to go back to the issue of client education.

Where did client education go?

Attentive readers will have noticed that I skipped a step in the chart in the last chapter. Where is the chapter on client education, the bit that comes in-between PR and marketing? There isn't a chapter on that, for some very good reasons.

The biggest reason is that I think that, as a profession, we have misunderstood client education, and so the best way to learn better client education strategies is to learn PR and marketing, since getting those two right will lead to better client education.

This links directly with a thread that has been developing through the entire book. For generations, interpreters have seen themselves as perfect neutral conduits, separate and aloof from what is going on around them. In the metaphor of that video from AIIC I mentioned back in Chapter 4, we are chefs who simply prepare exactly the same meal as the original speaker. Nowhere in that role are we asked to make sure no one has a fatal allergy or to determine whether the audience would prefer to eat with knives and forks. It's not our job.

That "it's not our job" aloofness easily translates into our approach to client education. Conference interpreters especially have a tendency to think that client education means convincing clients to do things the way that suits us. We can often tend towards automatically recommending traditional simultaneous interpreting, even when the job will just last an hour. We can see remote interpreting as too risky and so default to what we already know.

The same happens in other forms of interpreting. Historically, there have been certain ways of buying and organising court and medical and educational interpreting. Given the continued pressure to reduce rates and conditions in all of those areas, our default reaction is to oppose any and all changes that seem to present a risk to how we want things done.

And so it is not uncommon for interpreters to spend time trying to convince clients that the best thing to do is the thing we most want to do and the one that makes us feel comfortable. We might dress it up with other reasons, but clients can see through that.

Of course, standards are there for a reason. A couple of days before I wrote this, there was another disturbing story about interpreters suffering acoustic shock. We have to look after our own health and safety and accepted practices exist for a reason.

Even with all that in mind, client education shouldn't boil down to getting everyone to do it our way. Client education should mean working with clients to figure out the most effective (and cost-effective) way of delivering the results they need while ensuring good, safe and comfortable working conditions for the interpreters. Sometimes that will mean ISO booths; sometimes that will mean interpreting on-stage next to the speaker; sometimes it might even mean chuchotage. Client education isn't about forcing people's hands but helping them to learn as we achieve results *with* them – not *for* them, not against their will. We need to be delivering results *with* our clients.

Seeing interpreting as a partnership is the other thread that runs through this book and is the alternative to our traditional aloofness. Thinking through strategies to educate clients is only really useful if we do it through that lens. If we take the time to create targeted, relevant PR and build convincing marketing, we have already done most of the legwork needed for great client education. What does convincing marketing look like? Let's take a look.

How to fail at marketing

On my blog, there is a rather cheeky post. It is based on my experience of having people pitch their guest post ideas at me. Sadly, with the rare exception, most of them are awful. It's not that I know they are awful because I am some incredible marketing genius. Honestly, it feels as if I should be the last person to write this chapter. I know that those pitches are awful because I used to pitch like that.

If you read the post,[1] you will see that all of the pitches have the same issues – they aren't targeted to a specific person, there's no attempt to show relevance and they don't value people's time. While that post talked about pitching for guest blog posts and magazine articles, the same problems affect all of our marketing.

Let's start with websites. How well-targeted is your interpreter website, if you have one? Is it clear which kinds of companies you want to work with and who in the company should be reading your home page? Does it include only the information that is relevant to your target buyer? Is it succinct?

When I started out, I had no idea what any of that actually meant. Go back to the very first incarnation of my Integrity Languages website, built in 2011, after I realised that a ProZ.com profile wasn't going to be enough on its own, and you can see someone desperate to use keywords but without any idea of why or for whom.[2] In fact, even if you excuse the grey-on-grey design and the tautological front page, which informed you that on the site you would find exactly what you would expect to find on a website, the whole thing is an effective cure for insomnia.

I say all that knowing that a lot of interpreters, across all settings, might look at their own websites and see many of the same problems. None of us want to be generic, but few of us know any different and even fewer received any marketing training at university. We graduate and end up on our own, trying to run a business and keep on top of our interpreting skills at the same time. Most of us would rather we just had to do one of the two.

Oddly, in some cases, it's possible to forget marketing altogether. If you're a diplomatic interpreter in Brussels, a conference interpreter in Paris or Geneva or a medical interpreter in a country where your government actually offers decent rates, then all this marketing stuff might seem superfluous. It might even *be* superfluous. Yet I would implore you not to ignore this chapter.

While marketing might not be a commercial necessity for you right now, some of the issues this chapter covers will be relevant to you. Even if all your work is delivered on an ISO-standard silver platter by an obliging secretariat, you might find that you want to branch out into a new field one day. Even if you don't, you are probably on social media or might meet people who aren't interpreters. The way you interact with people in social media or real life can benefit from learning about marketing, even from someone like me who has learned everything he knows from doing it wrong.

Yes, I did just write that. If you are expecting that this chapter will go into the ins and outs of Facebook ads, social media strategy and complex referral systems, you will be disappointed. I am not an expert in any of them and would recommend reading books and blog posts by people like C. J. Hayden, Ewan Menzies, Judy and Dagmar Jenner, Julia Poger, and Pia Silva if you want to drill down into the nuts and bolts of individual marketing techniques.

Before we even get close to techniques like that, we need to think more clearly about our marketing approach and our marketing assumptions. Instead of giving you advice on certain tactics, which may or may not be valid by the time you get this book in your hands, I want to talk more about the way we view marketing and the assumptions that underlie it. Once we get that right, we can sort out our marketing messages. Once we get them right, we can start thinking through strategies and tactics.

It might be obvious that, at strategic moments in this book, I have turned to storytelling. This is another of those moments. To get ahold of exactly what I mean by marketing approaches, marketing assumptions and marketing messages, it helps to explain something of my marketing journey.

My marketing journey

It all seemed so easy. I live in Scotland, where most of the obvious interpreting work comes through three agencies whose names all start with the word "Global." There used to be a fourth agency that didn't use the word "Global," but they seem to have disappeared. Maybe they should have changed their name to "Global." With an agency-dominated market, the routine of getting work is fairly straight-forward, at least in theory. You email each of the agencies with a CV and wait. If you are very clever, you might get another interpreter to put in a good word for you, but that's about it.

After no interpreting turned up in the first six months after I started that process, I had landed some translation work. Still harbouring a deep-seated desire to make my money from sitting in a booth, I looked around for other ideas. I had vaguely heard that networking was a good idea so I went to a random local networking meeting I found in Glasgow, where I lived as a newly married man.

It was terrible. It was some kind of business show and I had no idea what to do, who to speak to or why they would be interested. I felt like a child who had accidentally found their way into a Victorian Gentlemen's club where they were talking about big important subjects while I was secretly wondering how long I had to stay.

I'm a fairly traditional extrovert, but this was hard work. It had been drummed into me that I should only interpret into my native language, and I could find no French speaker who might need me to interpret into English. Actually, I couldn't find any French speakers at all and didn't know what I would say to them even if I did find one. It didn't occur to me that they probably wouldn't be there if they needed an interpreter. Neither did it occur to me that, when people ask what you do, replying "whatever I get paid to do" is a really poor answer.

That one horrible networking experience sent me back home with my tail between my legs and led me to rely on a rather toxic mixture of replying to job ads on ProZ.com and translatorscafe.com and waiting by the phone for an agency to call. This was less "inbound marketing" and more "housebound marketing". It's little wonder that I would suffer a mental health episode after a couple of years, during which I spent an entire week staring at our bedroom wall and only leaving that pose to go to the toilet and eat the odd small thing.

For me, getting marketing wrong was as soul-destroying as it was career-destroying. The precise details of how that episode ended and how that led to me doing a PhD are a story for another book. What matters for this chapter is that the next important moment came around a year before I graduated from the PhD.

Even during the PhD, I could kind of rely on a flow of some work from a mixture of translation clients and the three interpreting agencies I spoke about earlier. Just as I was wrapping up the PhD and re-entering the full-time freelancer world, something fundamentally changed, and that change is still reverberating in my career to this day.

Having a modicum of success in academia and being invited to deliver guest lectures in three universities had loaded up my confidence, as had the increase in the number of calls I was receiving from those same three agencies. I didn't worry too much then, when one potential job ended up going nowhere. I simply chalked it up to experience and got on with life. When the second project disappeared, I was busy enough with PhD writing that it was a disappointment but not much more. Then the third assignment was cancelled and I lost the fourth over rates and then the fifth fell through as the end client decided to take it in-house, and I had to reject the sixth as the conditions were unacceptable. For six months, I went completely without interpreting work.

By the time I stood on the stage in the James Watt Centre of Heriot-Watt University, resplendent in my fuchsia gown to receive my PhD, I had rewritten my entire business strategy. The months before that had shown that I simply couldn't rely on work coming to me anymore. The agencies were no longer the reliable, if all too infrequent, source of work they had been, and it was becoming obvious that much of my translation work was becoming as much of a drag as it was an income source. I just wasn't enjoying it anymore.

I either had to give up and find myself a different job somewhere, perhaps hoping that academic careers weren't the hope-sucking treadmill that some people had told me they were, or I had to radically reshape my business. Welcoming a new child to the world in the December before I graduated had slowed my plans down somewhat, but by the spring of the next year, I was determined to make a go of winning direct clients. The daddy who shook the hand of the Chancellor before celebrating with some surprisingly good university buffet food was now also a businessman ready to win new clients.

Traditionally, this is the paragraph where I tout my newfound marketing credentials. I would love to tell you that, since that day, I have logged hundreds of interpreting days, built my business up to multimillion-pound empire and won prizes from foundations and associations across the globe. That would make a nice ending to my story and would make me feel much more comfortable about this chapter. It's always easier to write these things if you are someone who has made it.

I haven't made it yet. Some weeks I wonder even if I have made anything at all. As I mentioned earlier, if you want to read from the people who have it all sewn up, please do read everything you can from people like Julia Poger, Judy and Dagmar Jenner, Pia Silva, and Marta Stelmaszak. They know their stuff and really have made it.

There are some people, however, who are still in the place I am in. We still want and need more clients. We work outside of the giant markets where it really is possible to win assignments simply by having a working phone and a few connections. If you are working in a market where assignments can be spaced uncomfortably far apart and where most potential clients can't even spell 'interpreter', or its equivalent in your first language, this chapter will be helpful. In fact, having talked to a few interpreters in busier markets, they might find this chapter useful too. There are always new clients to win.

Learning to speak clientese

It will be no surprise to anyone who has read this far, but my first and most startling revelation was that all the words I previously used to speak about interpreting, like "accuracy," "neutrality" and even "conference interpreter" were all but meaningless to the other people I met when I went back to networking and started to visit trade shows. Even the word "multilingual" fell on deaf ears.

Here's a simple example. In the UK, a decent proportion of conferences are run by overworked personal assistants. I spotted that market and decided that, since I had a bit of writing under my belt by then, I would pitch an article to the editor of a leading magazine for personal assistants. The title was something like "Successful multilingual events." A couple of weeks later, I received a polite reply telling me that the topic wasn't within their remit. To my shock, less than a week later, someone else would have an article appear in the magazine talking about "international events," covering much the same ground as I would have but without any mention of interpreting.

One word, one single, solitary word was the difference between getting in front of thousands of potential buyers and having my email become a premature victim of Inbox Zero. Since I didn't want to waste any more time, I decided to switch into listening mode, attending client events, networking with other businesses and working with business coaches.

All that work taught me a marketing approach that I still use today. Whichever medium I am using, I go straight to the issues and pain points affecting my potential clients and don't even mention rates or booths or language regimes until the time is right. Instead of starting by dropping a rulebook on the table, I start by finding out as much as I can about the client, their event and their needs. I even wrote a standard brief to get all that down on one sheet of paper.[3] That saves them time and saves me hassle.

As I began to learn to see things from the point of view of potential clients, I also realised how tricky it can be to get the right information if you are a buyer. Yes, we can all point to websites and fact sheets, but since many potential clients don't even know the difference between a translator and an interpreter, we can't really expect them to know that AIIC are a good source or that they can download the "Interpreting: Getting it Right" help sheet from various professional associations, especially when those particular pages rarely score high on Google. Many buyers prefer to go on word-of-mouth recommendations anyway.

Learning to speak clientese led me to a further discovery. Potential clients rarely attend translation and interpreting conferences. We need to go to them.

Becoming a client anthropologist

Using the right words wasn't enough. It got me into conversations and helped me understand more of how and why clients bought interpreting, but it was only the first step. The more business events I attended where I was the only interpreter in the room, the more I learned about business. The more I learned about business, the more I began to focus on just the right events and just the most useful training. The more I did that, the more I saw the world through the eyes of potential clients.

By attending client events and doing training with them, I picked up some interesting information. Every industry has its own quirks. Learning those quirks makes marketing much easier.

Here's a simple example. In September 2016, I was flying down to Birmingham, on my way to another board meeting of the Institute of Translation and Interpreting. As usual, I was flying with regional airline FlyBe and, as usual, I was bored enough and curious enough to flick through their flight magazine. I was reading the business section and read a few international business success stories. Yet I noticed that no one mentioned interpreting.

I grabbed an app on my phone and took a picture of the editor's email address and articles that seemed most relevant. Still 25,000 feet above central England, I drafted a quick email. As soon as I hit the ground and had stable, free Wi-Fi, I checked my email for typos and sent it off. A few months and a bit of chasing later, I sat on a very similar flight, reading a two-page article with my happy face at the end of it.

That isn't the end of the story. Since the magazine is published online as well as in print, I took the opportunity to share the article on every social media channel I could find, as well as just about every Facebook group that was even vaguely connected to translation and interpreting. I thought it would be an encouragement to others.

What I didn't realise was that it would be spotted by a small, very good translation agency who were looking for a consultant interpreter to cover a small event put on by one of their favourite clients, a very large and important luxury brand. Assuming that I might know something about interpreting, given that I had just appeared in an inflight magazine, they offered me the assignment, which I took. A few months later, I was interpreting in London for some serious bigwigs.

The process of winning that article and the subsequent assignment have been repeated since then. The steps are always the same. The process always has to start with discovering what clients actually want. This could be an editor desperate for content, a business looking to export, a scientist looking to share a discovery, a teacher trying to communicate effectively with Deaf pupils or a hundred other things. Understanding this need and being able to talk about it in language that is meaningful for your potential client takes away a lot of the bidding and struggle from marketing.

Looking for this information will sadly eliminate a lot of potential clients too. Some potential clients just want everything done quickly or cheaply. Other potential clients just want to put on nice corporate events with not a hint of another language in sight. Still other clients will want services that you don't offer and don't want to touch.

Being brave enough to discover what clients really want and need reduces stress and wasted time but confronts us with the unfortunate reality that not everyone we think needs interpreters will ever want to buy our services. Even then, some clients who both need and want interpreting will only be interested in getting everything as quickly and cheaply as possible. While protesting and attempting to change their minds might seem noble, it rarely works. If anything, it just makes us look angry or desperate.

The next step is figuring out how clients want to be contacted. I have had some potential clients who are only interested in phone calls and won't give away any useful information in emails. Others have wanted a face-to-face coffee meeting. It's hard to figure out in advance which method will work. Being just as comfortable writing a posh quote on headed notepaper before posting it express delivery as we are giving prices on the phone with an email confirmation is going to become a vital skill for interpreters. Oddly enough, now that pretty much everyone is on social media, you make more of an impression being able to use other means of communication well.

Lastly in the marketing process, and this is where I am still having to learn the hard way, following up and heading towards a sale is an artform. I am no great salesperson and am having to learn when to go for a seventh round of follow-up emails and when to leave the client and go play with my kids instead. There are lots of good books on turning marketing interest to solid sales and interpreters will need to become familiar with them to survive.

Marketing when you don't feel like it

In all this process, I have learned some pretty hard lessons. Some "dream clients" are going to turn out to be impossible to win. Some high potential partnerships will go to mega agencies who farm the work out to whoever answers their emails first. Sometimes you will spend hundreds of pounds to attend an event and find that it was as useful as attending a three-day seminar on underwater cricket.

The hardest lesson of all for me to learn was that marketing interpreting in a way that really demonstrates its value to clients means being consistent. You can attend a great tradeshow on Monday and gather hundreds of business cards from excited connections, but if you can't keep in contact with them and can't find a way to show even more people that interpreting really matters and can make a difference to their business, you won't get very far.

Unless we can commit to setting aside regular marketing time, our marketing efforts won't succeed. That article in a magazine won me a new client but I got so enamoured with that single achievement that I missed lots of opportunities to build on it. Doing a few small things consistently well adds up to more benefits than going viral for a week and then doing nothing afterwards.

I've had to learn to do something marketing related, even when I don't feel like it. My approach to marketing might feature attending big events and trying to win big articles, but those efforts are shored up with consistently adding interesting potential clients on LinkedIn, sending follow-up emails to people I meet, creating engaging content to help clients work more effectively with interpreters and sending quick responses when helpful people tag me in Facebook groups aimed at my target clients.

Little things done consistently and done as well as I can – that's what I am trying to keep doing. Sure, there are thousands of coaches offering instant success if you buy this course or buy this other book but getting the small things right seems far more attuned to what interpreters actually do anyway. Besides, as interpreters, we are in the business of listening to people and speaking in a way that they understand. Our marketing should reflect that.

Notes

1   https://www.integritylanguages.co.uk/2017/07/20/how-to-fail-at-pitching/.
2   http://bit.ly/IntegLangs2011.
3   You can download it from this page: http://bit.ly/UIB-Integlangs.

Chapter 12

Deliver more than words

In many cases, the success of an event, business deal or medical appointment hinges on the interpreter's expertise and decision-making. In those environments, tiny decisions make a big difference. Do you explain a term or keep it as is? What do you do with that joke? What do you do if the parties misunderstand each other?

Good interpreting is the ability to take such decisions intelligently. The truth is that even if we want to keep using the traditional definition of interpreters as being impartial, accurate and terminologically exact, there will always be decisions we take as to how to solve specific problems. Those decisions are rarely clear-cut.

Those paragraphs are taken word-for-word from the first chapter of this book. By this point, their significance should be even greater than it was earlier. In a world where it is entirely possible that machines can be developed to deliver interpreting that portrays *what* was said in another language, even if the ability to convey *how* it was said is highly debatable, the position and prestige of human interpreters would seem to be under threat.

To the extent that we view the ideal of interpreting as the perfectly impartial delivery of linguistic content, it is indeed under threat. To write anything else would mean ignoring everything we have seen so far about the progress of speech translation and the potential of the algorithms behind it.

Accepting the view that machines might one day produce an impartial delivery of content from one language to another is not the same as forecasting the demise of human interpreting – far from it. It simply means that the livelihoods of human interpreters are only under threat if they produce conduit model interpreting. Put even more succinctly, machines will only replace interpreters who interpret like machines.

If human interpreters want to keep their jobs, we need to do even more than mastering our own PR and marketing interpreting in a way that speaks to the needs and wants our prospective clients really have. If we want to survive and thrive in the age of speech translation, we have to do jobs that machines can't do and the technologists who build them don't understand. It's time to become consultants.

Consultant interpreters, but not as we knew them

If you haven't heard of consultant interpreters, it's worth a quick refresher course. In many interpreting markets, especially conference and business interpreting in Europe, there are interpreters who don't just interpret but who build teams of interpreters, advise clients on decisions such as which interpreting mode will work best and liaise with equipment suppliers.

These professionals are interpreters but also recruiters, marketers, salespeople, administrators and advisors. That much is common practice, but I recently came across a whole new angle on the role.

I had the honour of coaching two sign language interpreters during their six-month internships with Police Scotland and the National Health Service in Greater Glasgow and Clyde, as part of a project led by Prof Graham Turner at Heriot-Watt University and sponsored by the Scottish Government Equality Unit. On one occasion, the interns were visiting a prison, accompanied by a staff member. On their tour, they were shown the glass-walled rooms where prisoners received their advocacy visits. During the chat, it became clear that these rooms were unfit for Deaf prisoners as they use a visio-spatial language – any sign language user nearby would be able to understand everything that was being said. The staff member realised this wouldn't work and started working on alternative arrangements.

One visit, one realisation, the beginning of a small but important change in an organisation. The presence of two interpreters and a short conversation planted a seed for an important improvement in the services available to an already vulnerable group. What difference can you make in your conversations with clients?

Interpreters as advocates?

At this point, some readers will be very wary. Is this a not-so-subtle call for interpreters to become advocates? Am I arguing that unless interpreters become walking human rights activists, we are heading for professional oblivion?

Actually, the answer to both of those questions is a qualified no. Let's start with why the answer is "no" before qualifying why the question isn't quite as straightforward as it seems.

If what we mean by becoming advocates is that interpreters should ditch or minimise their linguistic function and push for the rights of one of the parties they are interpreting for over the other, I would want to wave a big red danger flag. Even at the most amoral, mercenary level, we forget who pays us at our peril. We cannot expect to be paid by a system, whether that's a government bureaucracy or a large enterprise, while we try to break or subvert it. It might sound ironically clever on paper, but it is a one-way ticket to losing our jobs. Governments and administrations may be imperfect, but they have a job to do. We will only advance our cause by helping those systems run more effectively and more fairly, not by trying to weaken them.

If we want to be full-time advocates, we can always change jobs to do that. If we want to make sure that every meeting we work at runs more effectively and achieves its aim, we'll be heading in the right direction.

Where advocacy is a useful, albeit coloured, term is in the fact that it reminds us that interpreting often involves power imbalances and those power imbalances can turn a straightforward assignment into an incomprehensible mess. Take the business negotiation I discussed way back in Chapter 1. To begin with, the greatest power imbalance was between the primary participants, who were all trained, experienced experts in that area, and their interpreter, who was well prepared and ready but hadn't spent his entire working life around the equipment being bought and sold. This power imbalance was made obvious within a few minutes of the assignment starting, when the French buyer announced to everyone in the room in perfectly clear French, "I could do this in English but I don't want to."

Add into the mix that the CEO of the British company informed me at the end of the meeting that he understood everything that was said in French (but couldn't follow what was happening), and you have a cocktail potent enough to cause any interpreter to slip up. Yet by the time the delegates had marched out of the negotiating room and down the corridor, the power had shifted. The most powerful person in the corridor, even if just for a moment, was the interpreter. I didn't gain that power by sudden acquisition of expertise or by usurping the clients but because of one tiny difference between interpreters and their clients. While they were locked into what they were trying to accomplish as individuals in that moment, working as an interpreter made me sensitive to what was going on in the meeting as a whole.

I'm sure almost all interpreters have been in that place. We catch little body language cues and read bobbing backs of heads. We pick up repetition and strained voices. We notice hesitations, pauses and responses that are unrelated to what was said previously. We spot when people aren't understanding and when cultural expectations are preventing them from saying what they need to say. We can see objections about to arise and spot upcoming fights at 50 paces.

We have to do all this to separate irony from seriousness, joking from goading, fear from excitement, confusion from troublemaking, despair from apathy and attention from vagueness. We literally cannot faithfully produce what was said and how and why it was said without being able to do that complex processing of emotions and intentions. Being aware of the small indicators of mood, comprehension and discomfort is the hallmark of a human interpreter; knowing how to use that knowledge might just be the key to our future.

If we see advocacy as a buzzword that gets us thinking about the fact that we are always active participants when we interpret, it might have its uses. Sure, talking about triadic interpreting is less problematic and talking about our agency is more descriptive, but if the advocacy debate is some kind of shortcut to being more aware of what we do and debating what we *might* do, it's a debate worth having.

The smart interpreter

While I am not making a bold push for interpreters to become advocates, I am suggesting that with automatic speech translation heading from buggy annoyance to useful tool, human interpreters have to move from expensive necessity to invaluable partner. From the moment clients start thinking about chatting to people who don't speak their language to the final count of the return on investment of their hard work, interpreters should be in the loop, listening to requirements and concerns, giving sage advice on delivery, working with suppliers and organisers, ensuring best practice, building collaborations and teams, selecting technology, learning, growing and creating space for learning and growth among their clients too.

If that all sounds abstract or divorced from everyday reality, it might help to break it up. In the rest of this chapter, I want to go through what it looks like for interpreters to deliver more than words at different stages of the process. Since we are all used to talking about the rights and wrongs of what we do while we interpret, it makes sense to start there, before working outwards and backwards, to areas like strategy and influencing, which we don't know so well.

Delivering more than words – in the moment

What sort of interpreting can we deliver in the moment that will set us apart from even the best content delivered from our digital pseudo-replacements? To figure that out, we only need to return to the way in which speech translation works.

Speech translation is based entirely on the words that are said. There is no space within its algorithms or data for intonation, intention, tone of voice or context. It's as if a speech was suddenly written down, with all other clues and cues destroyed. Is Martin Luther King's "I have a dream" speech as persuasive as a piece of prose for someone who knows nothing of its history and context? Is anyone who knows nothing about the Cold War or the post-war history of Europe in any way affected by seeing the words "Mr Gorbachev, tear down this wall" in print?

We might talk about "identifying with the speaker" and Daniel Gile might have said that interpreters should be the speaker's *"alter ego"* (2009, p. 34), but we haven't always reflected this idea in the ways we speak about interpreting. Even more importantly, it's all too easy, with our commitment to professional neutrality, to find ourselves delivering content with all the verve and vigour of a tired tortoise.

We are trained to attend to the language part of what is said and to deverbalise meaning but we forget at our peril that meaning is not just about words but how they are used in a context. In short, even with all the cognitive pressures we have discussed and even with all the difficulties we face in doing our jobs at all, we have to aim higher than simply being accurate.

I distinctly remember the treat of hearing two of my Italian colleagues, Stefania Ricci and Alessandra MacKenzie, interpret a technically challenging yet highly emotive session on the clear up after a marine accident. Their performance was not just a masterclass in how to be superb relay interpreters but showcased even better public speaking and vocal skills than the original speakers.

When the speakers gave us precise technical details of the procedures they used, Alessandra and Stefania found just the right level of English terminology. When the speakers described the scene and the challenges they faced, we felt that we were there too. When they expressed their satisfaction at a hard job well done, it was as if we could sigh with contentment with them.

There was no doubt in my mind or in the minds of the audience members that their performance could not have been even approached by any machine. For 30 minutes, Alessandra and Stefania got inside the heads of the speakers and the audience and gave us not just accuracy but emotion, clarity and beauty. Even technical presentations can sound beautiful with the right interpreters.

Obviously, emotion, clarity and beauty are not always the required criteria for interpreting. Sometimes precision, concision and directness are needed. Other times, we will need empathy, understanding and cultural awareness. Whatever the skills we need, we can no longer get away with anything less than throwing our all into interpreting. We can't afford to be anything less than (temporary) field experts, strong public speakers, compassionate thinkers and committed partners.

In the doctor's office, delivering more than words will mean not "just interpreting" between German and English or between Nahuatl and Spanish but interpreting in such a way that a patient who doesn't understand anything of the system they are visiting can express themselves as clearly and get the same level of treatment as someone who has lived in the city all their lives and went to school with the doctors.

In the conference hall, delivering more than words means ensuring that the speakers are at least as convincing in French or Dutch or Danish or English as they were in whatever language they spoke from the podium. It will mean interpreting so effectively that clients begin to see multilingual conferences as the default and monolingual conferences as a poor, limited, second choice.

If that sounds impossible, I would recommend listening to the episode of the Troublesome Terps podcast on English as a *lingua franca*. There, experienced researcher and interpreter trainer Karin Reithofer explained that many interpreters see the rise of English as a threat to their livelihoods, and many clients see it as a route to avoid paying for interpreting. Yet in her research (Reithofer, 2010, 2013) she found strong evidence that interpreting users remember far more when hearing interpreting into their native language than they do in second-language English. Instead of English as a *lingua franca* being a threat, she now sees it as an opportunity to explain to clients the value of what we do for them and how we make a difference. Effective interpreting is interpreting that makes clients sit up and take notice. In fact, visiting a recent conference on the international events industry convinced me that clients are indeed beginning to realise that people learn better in their first language (Downie, 2019).

In the court system, delivering more than words will mean nothing less than working towards the day when everyone gets the same access to justice and the same ability to have their say in court, no matter which language they speak. Here, possibly unlike any other area, we might actually have to start pushing against established practice and existing bias outside of the interpreting environment in order to allow us to perform adequately within it. The existing legal fiction of assuming that the interpreter can and does perfectly produce an exact rendition of what was originally said without any explanations, restructuring or intervention will need to be reviewed. Perhaps that legal fiction is what lies behind the assumption by people like the Lord Chief Justice that interpreters can be replaced by machines.

We all know that great interpreting in the moment doesn't happen on its own. It takes practice, expertise, courage and skill. It takes a lot of things that we will examine a little later, but first, it's important to really get to grips with its main features, even if this will look slightly different in every situation.

The main feature of interpreting that delivers more than words is just that: it delivers more than words. We have to get used to quickly figuring out how to find a way of turning English intonation shifts into French sentence structure, allusions to poetry in Chinese into German that fits the context and Spanish idioms into Finnish thinking. This does not necessarily mean washing any sense of foreignness out of the speeches and conversations we interpret, but it does mean learning the contextually correct way to handle, say, irony or a culture-specific joke or an implied accusation.

I would dearly love to write a once-and-for-all-time guide to what great interpreting looks like or sounds like, but things aren't that easy. When interpreting in church, for a speaker whom I know is monolingual and doesn't mean to offend, I might lengthen my lag and soften the impact of tough questions that work well in his home country but would turn off a French audience. If I was interpreting for the same speaker in front of an audience of world-travelling leaders, I probably wouldn't. If you are interpreting for a Deaf person who didn't have the opportunity of post-secondary education and is visiting a lawyer, you will probably use different techniques than those you would use for a Deaf university professor coming up for the annual review.

In fact, there should be no "probably" about it. The only interpreters who will survive the rise of speech translation are those who are able to precisely tune their interpreting to the situations in which they work. You might have been trained for international diplomacy and the rigours of EU policy, but if the only work you can get is in scientific conferences, learning the interpreting that clients need and appreciate there is vital. Experienced clients really can tell the difference between a really good job and mediocre service.

Instead of telling you what interpreting that delivers more than words might look like in your situation, it seems to make more sense for me to ask you. In your situations, for your clients, with their concerns and pressures and goals, what does it look like and feel like for you to deliver interpreting so good that they wouldn't even dream of bringing in a machine?

Hopefully, everyone reading this has experienced the joy of having at least one client who was overjoyed at the service we delivered. To find out what it means to deliver more than words, we need to study those clients, understand them and turn that knowledge into concrete decisions in the booth, in the doctor's surgery and in the court – in short, wherever we work.

Preparing to deliver more than words

While every interpreter might recognise the warm smile of a very happy client, it's too easy to forget how we got to that point. Rolling out old clichés such as, "You have to fulfil client needs" or "Know what your client really wants" is as boring as it is insulting. The truth is that client-pleasing performance in an interpreting event tends to be related to excellent preparation beforehand.

This doesn't just mean being on top of terminology knowledge, gathering as much information as you can about the event and practising by listening to the speakers. To deliver excellent interpreting, we need to understand the background to the event, including how it fits with the rest of the work done by the client, understand the goals of the event and be sharp enough with our skills to deliver what's needed in the moment.

The last of those three requirements is closely linked to the chapter on Continued Professional Development (CPD) in my first book, *Being a Successful Interpreter: Adding Value and Delivering Excellence*. In my own work as an interpreter and in the work I recently completed with intern interpreters, it has become clear that sustained, targeted interpreting practice outside of the work is key. Small choices such as journaling each assignment to look for patterns in our delivery, recording a short test speech to check our vocal quality and intonation and working with a partner to practice our skills can make a big difference in our performance. Since coaching interns, I have been more aware of how helpful it is to work on verbal fluency, multitasking and my familiarity with the ways in which my native and working language are used by native speakers.

It's not always easy to make time for CPD, and there is always the temptation to work more to make more money or even, in many situations, to work long hours just to pay the bills. There is another way. If we can improve our rates and our clients to even buy ourselves as little as one day a month, we can work hard to improve our skills.

CPD can be anything from attending training aimed at our clients to working on our consecutive interpreting techniques. We need to start strategically thinking about the skills we need to consistently deliver interpreting that makes a difference. For medical interpreters, this absolutely means doing some kind of medical training. For court interpreters, this means taking a course in some area of law. For sign language interpreters, this means keeping up with what researchers are learning about Deaf culture and staying plugged in to your local Deaf community.

Before an assignment is even offered to us, we need to have the background and profile to make clients interested in our skills to solve their problems. The interpreter who has a degree in engineering alongside their interpreting degree will likely make a better interpreter at a factory tour than the qualified interpreter who spent three days in YouTube videos and term lists. The second interpreter might know the terms, but the first one has lived them. Believe it or not, there is good research to prove that, too. My first officemate at Heriot-Watt University was a researcher by the name of Gao Wei. He showed that interpreters who had bodily experience of a task before interpreting a speech on it outperformed those who prepared the traditional way (Gao, 2011). Perhaps we need to try winning our own direct clients and daring to ask for a tour before we interpret in the factory. We could look to gain specialist hands-on training in police interview techniques before doing an interview or pay for a few counselling sessions of our own before interpreting at one.

All this is a long way of saying that specialism may become a necessity across the profession. Yes, there are already specialist court and medical interpreters, but at least in the UK, conference interpreters tend to be generalists by accident, if not by design, and business interpreters can find themselves in meetings ranging from disciplinary hearings to contract negotiations. We can all make the arguments about having to make ends meet, and few of us can afford to turn down a good assignment, but perhaps we would stand a better chance of winning contracts ourselves and leaving cheaper suppliers behind if we could stand in front of clients knowing that we had a level of real expertise in their area.

If this sounds impossible, we can take inspiration from our colleagues in the world of translation. There, Chris Durban has been arguing for years that translators should be comfortable sitting in board meetings with clients and being able to discuss issues with them in their language and using the logic they understand. David Jemielity has gone one step further. As the Head of Translation for Banque Cantonale Vaudoise in Switzerland, he has built a translation department that regularly works closely with those writing the source texts to make sure that the entire communication process works. Is it so outlandish to imagine interpreters being similarly respected by their clients? Should we forever banish ourselves for fear of overstepping our roles or will the rise of the robots galvanise us to use every skill we have to deliver exceptional value to clients?

A few years ago, I bought the book *Power to Create* by Tim Redmond. In it he talks about the difference between the scarcity mindset and the abundance mindset. Independent of any economic or political situation, people with the scarcity mindset see only difficulties and obstructions. To them, there are always reasons to feel bleak about the future. Every time someone else is successful, it makes them jealous. Every time a client goes for a cheaper option, they see it as presaging the day when their job will fly away like a piece of junk mail in a tornado. People with the abundance mindset, whether they work in a struggling economy or a thriving one, see things differently. According to him, these people are actively attracted to problems, as they see them as the opportunity to create value. For them, making money isn't the bottom line – creating value is.

According to Tim Redmond, creating value by actively seeking problems and solving them is the key to business. If we chase money, we will find ourselves in a never-ending race to the bottom. If we look to create value by solving problems, the money naturally follows. Applied to interpreting, this means seeing our role as not just delivering excellent interpreting in the event but understanding what problems interpreting solves for clients. Even more, it means understanding the wider context in which we deliver interpreting and thinking through how we can use our other skills (cultural awareness, public speaking, research, organisation, to name but a few) to help clients solve wider problems. Perhaps we could run training sessions for speakers on doing successful speeches in multicultural meetings. Perhaps we could offer clients advice on how to get the most from interpreting: which meetings really need us and which meetings could be done without us. Certainly, putting value first means marketing and selling interpreting in ways that are much more compelling than writing "five years of experience in the medical sector, master's degree from XXXX University."

On top of all that, of course, we still have to be experts in the regular kinds of preparation that many of us are used to. Storing useful terminology, understanding the purpose of an event and getting ready to interpret speakers with a range of accents should be home turf for any good interpreter. Delivering interpreting that matters means understanding that speakers will have strong accents, crack jokes, allude to incidents we have no clue about, overrun their slots and speak in their second, third or fourth languages. Learning to expect these things and deliver excellently even when they do happen will set apart the interpreters clients want to work with from the ones clients try to avoid. None of these things happen because clients want to wind up interpreters. They're just part of running an international event. The sooner we accept that and work out how to deliver better results than clients expect despite all that, the better things will go.

Client care that delivers more than words

Getting all this right relies on interpreters really understanding and caring about their clients. From the moment we first come into contact with a potential client to the last time they ever hear from us, clients need to know that we care about what they care about and they need to be reassured that we will deliver when they need us to.

It all starts from the first time clients ever hear about us. Two quick stories will serve to show how to get this right and how to get it wrong. Let's start with the time it went wrong.

I was visiting some stands at a tradeshow and had had a pretty good day. I knew there were some colleagues there too, but I hadn't managed to meet up with them for various reasons. I got to one stand and the conversation went like this.

"Hi, nice to meet you. I'm Jonathan."

"What are you selling?"

"Actually, I'm here to see what kinds of events you do."

"We do lots of events, from corporate days out to big conferences. What kind of business are you in?"

"I build interpreting teams for international events."

"Oh no. You're not one of those *interpreters* are you? We told them we don't do international events and we are tired of being sold to by interpreters."

"I'm really sorry to hear that. Thanks for the chat anyway."

Ouch. To this day, I have no idea what, if anything, those colleagues said or did to put the people on the stand on such a defensive posture. It could be that the folks on the stand were just tired or rude but their reaction to finding out I was an interpreter was shocking. It was shocking enough to get me to re-evaluate my own approach to the conference and check whether I was pushing people away too.

Sadly, there are some natural interpreter behaviours that put clients off, and those will be different for each client. Some clients will want to get down to business right away; others will want a coffee or a lunch meeting. Some clients will want us to keep in touch; others will want us to go away and stay away. Being genuinely friendly and interested in their business is usually the safest approach.

Thankfully, not all experiences are like the one I had at that show. In fact, one of my favourite networking events, a business lunch called Curry Connections, once showed me just how good a reception we can get. The lunch happens once a month on a Friday and this particular month, I was running late as I had been tidying the proposal for a book that needed to be sent to a certain international publisher. I walked in and got the usual friendly greeting from the host. That greeting, however, was vastly overwhelmed by the greeting I got from a local business consultant when I sat down.

"Jonathan," he boomed. "Great to see you. You know, Steve here was just talking to me about a language problem he has in his business and I told him that you were the man to talk to as you are our resident languages expert. Steve, meet Jonathan. He's the guy I told you about. He'll sort it."

Wow. To this day, I have no idea what I did, if anything, to earn such a dazzling introduction. It could be that he was just in an exceptionally good mood. It could be that he genuinely thought I could fix anything vaguely language-related. It was shocking enough to get me to re-evaluate how I network and what in my own manner and approach might be making someone so ready to recommend my services.

Helpfully, there are some natural interpreter behaviours that get clients excited and make them more likely to work with us. Showing genuine interest in their business, asking interesting questions, not forcing ourselves on them – these are all both good business and good people skills. We might expect all interpreters to have great people skills but sadly, they aren't always on display. It's absolutely right for clients to judge us based on their impressions of meeting us in person. Many of them are going to pay to hire us to work in person anyway. Being approachable and warm will do us many favours.

Before we even get to the nitty-gritty of setting up an individual assignment, we need to keep giving off the aura of approachable expert. Responding to emails promptly, even if just via an out-of-office message, keeping clients up to date when processes take time and giving useful information and helpful hints will all help keep the relationship strong. One shortcut I have found is to create a one-page briefing document which clients can fill in, so we have all the information we need in one place.[1] Showing that you care about client time by explaining that you use that brief to reduce long email conversations and help them gather their thoughts will always make a good impression. The side effect of being able to prepare more effectively isn't bad either.

If you are thinking that we really shouldn't need to talk about the basics of responding to emails promptly, being gracious and keeping people up to date then you have had better experiences than I have. From the point of view of someone who builds interpreting teams, I could tell you strange stories of interpreters disappearing into the aether, direct questions getting vague responses and people getting annoyed when you push for a response so you can send a quote. Equally, I could recount cases where colleagues have gone above and beyond the call of duty to deliver excellent information and superb interpreting. I know which colleagues I can rely on and which I will go to only when absolutely necessary. If we know that, what makes us think that clients won't get wise too?

I also have to admit to having dropped the ball on occasion, being guilty of taking too long to respond and forgetting to send updates. We all make mistakes, but what matters is learning from them and doing better the next time the opportunity comes up. Someone who makes a small mistake and learns from it is better than an arrogant person who believes that they have done everything correctly. The question will always be "What are we doing to improve what we deliver?"

More than words in a few words

This chapter has deliberately gone into lots of examples. In doing so, it might have seemed to veer between retelling the obvious and suggesting the impossible. While I really do believe and try to practice all of the suggestions in this chapter, what matters is not the specific ideas or approaches but the overall view we take of our own work and the way we relate to clients. Perhaps the greatest reason that speech translation has been so attractive to some people is that they promise easy, instant interpreting. While we can't and shouldn't offer that, we can become aware of the challenges that poses for us.

When I started out, being an interpreter was quite a lot like having a shop in a busy main street. So long as you were there and were known enough, eventually someone would buy something. It didn't particularly matter if you were a brand name or a discount supplier. There was enough footfall and there were enough clients that there was a good chance that someone would pick you for something. Walk through any main street in the UK and you can see that times have changed. Practically every town and city in the country has more boarded-up shopfronts than ever before and even established names are struggling to keep pace with online retailers.

Outside of the giant interpreting markets, interpreters find themselves in a similar situation. Our field is more competitive than ever, even before interpreting bots and apps are thrown in. The interpreters who want to thrive could benefit by learning from the shops that are thriving. In the UK, apart from cutting costs to drastically low levels, the shops that are growing have some combination of excellent customer service, unique products and a reputation for innovation. People who do shop in city centres want a unique experience and products they just can't get anywhere else. The interpreters who succeed by delivering more than words will have to shed the aloof image that interpreters sometimes get and deliver not just amazing interpreting but leading client service and an enjoyable experience for clients. Even our amazing interpreting will need to become increasingly specialist.

The clients who aren't just fishing for another quote, before they will go with their mates anyway, often see their meeting as hard or specialist. It might be high-risk or just an important day on their calendar. If it's the same old rotating board meeting they run every year, with the same agenda since 1962, then we should expect them to try to get prices down. If this is their big chance to crack a new market or impress the regulators or win that new contract, we should know that they need more than the assurance that six interpreters will turn up and do the job. They want and feel they need experts and specialists whose interpreting is worth hundreds of times more than they are likely to pay.

We sometimes joke about clients who need "hand-holding" and to be guided through the process, but often it is those clients who turn out to be the most valuable. Using that "hand-holding" process to really dig under the skin of what the clients are trying to achieve would not just make our lives easier but impress the clients, too.

In a world covered in tech gadgets to automate processes, maybe the greatest thing we have to sell is precisely our humanity. Your smartphone couldn't care less whether the texts it spits out win you a new contract or leaves you stuck in the middle of a field. Machines can't ever "get it" – but humans can. And when clients know we "get it," we find that we get their respect and get treated better, too.

Note

1   You can download a blank version here: http://bit.ly/UIB-Integlangs.

References

Downie, J. 2019, *Confex and the future of international events, integrity languages.* <https://www.integritylanguages.co.uk/2019/04/11/confex-and-the-future-of-international-events/>.

Gao, W. 2011, *Coherence in simultaneous interpreting: an idealized cognitive model perspective*, Thesis, Heriot-Watt University. <https://www.ros.hw.ac.uk/handle/10399/2504>.

Gile, D. 2009, *Basic concepts and models for interpreter and translator training*, John Benjamins Publishing Company, Amsterdam.

Reithofer, K. 2010, 'English as a lingua franca vs. interpreting: battleground or peaceful coexistence?', *The Interpreters' Newsletter*, no. 15, pp. 143–157.

Reithofer, K. 2013, 'Comparing modes of communication: the effect of English as a lingua franca vs. interpreting', *Interpreting*, vol. 15, no. 1, pp. 48–73.

Chapter 13

Coaching and supervision

It had been an unimaginably long day. For the only time in my career, I had started work at an interpreting assignment at 9:00 a.m., and after longer breaks than usual the last session had ended at 7:00 p.m., with dinner ending an hour later. While those are long hours, a lunchtime nap and those long breaks made them relatively bearable. Yet here I was, sitting in the hotel room feeling emotionally spent. It wasn't the length of the work, although the work was long. It wasn't the difficulty of the work, although using three interpreting modes within any three-hour period is a challenge in itself. It was the nature of the work. During that day, I had heard and interpreted real-life stories that shook me.

And so there I was, at a shade after 8:00 p.m., sitting in the hotel room, feeling unable to think much beyond the comforting act of getting a cup of tea. Confidentiality prevents me from sharing the stories, but I can say that they told of people losing what they held dear and somehow having to find a way through. Even the people telling them sometimes mentioned that they had spared us the worst.

As a conference interpreter, I have it easy. While I might hit those stories once or twice a year, at the most, my colleagues in medical and legal interpreting will deal with them on a normal day. One colleague once told me how she had dealt with three heartbreaking medical assignments in the same day and then found herself unable to get up the next morning.

It's all very well for me to write about the need to see our humanity as an advantage over the machines, but at times – when we hit emotional content or deal with heartbreaking assignments – that very humanity can seem like a weakness. Machines don't cry. We do.

Yet in those situations, in those difficult and heartbreaking assignments, we paradoxically find that we, weak and fragile humans, are exactly the right people for the job. Sometimes it's just the right thing to have an interpreter who can relay the very emotions coursing through the speaker. To have a calm, quasi-robotic voice telling stories of loss would be an insult.

Having emotions is important, understanding how to accept and process them and learning to make good, ethical decisions while in heightened emotional states is vital. I was blessed that evening to have the support of a loving wife who understood my need to hear a voice outside of that assignment. It also helped to have a way of contacting an expert who trains mental health nurses and who is happy for me to send the odd "is this normal?" message.

If this was a normal research book, or even following the same model as my first book, this is the point where I would pull out lots of references and talk through the latest research. There are indeed lots of excellent references. I could talk about how Robyn Dean and Robert Pollard have demonstrated the power of case conferencing (Dean and Pollard, 2009). I could discuss how, yet again, sign language researchers are leading the way by pushing for clinical supervision to be included as standard in interpreter training and practice (Dean, Pollard Jr and English, 2004; Hetherington, 2012). I could even tell stories of meeting Dr Jules Dickinson, an interpreter trained as an interpreter supervisor. If I wanted to, I could discuss the difference between clinical supervision and line management.

Those are all great things to discuss and a little Googling will take you to excellent discussions by leading experts. The problem is that, as interpreters, we are used to reading lots of information, skimming for the important bits and then moving on. Since we are all trained to do quick research, extract key terms and summarise long messages in short snippets, the danger is that, if I were to write in the typical way, I doubt many people would take it onboard. Some people would, of course, but for others, this would just be another chapter.

Instead, I want to take a different tack entirely. The rest of this chapter will be split into two sections. In the first, I want to write an entreaty, a plea of sorts, for us to take our own mental health and support structures more seriously. I will write it as an interpreter who has experienced what it is like to have to deal with some of the mental health risks of being an interpreter and as a researcher who looks to approach everything with critical thinking. The second section will turn from supervision to coaching in order to discuss the importance of working on our skills in a strategic fashion, with someone who can check up on our progress. There are some really nice coaching models in existence already, and one of them is sure to work for you.

Who's got your back?

In a previous chapter, I mentioned the project I recently worked on, where a team of us examined how to integrate sign language interpreters into the police and NHS and how to help newly graduated sign language interpreters transition from training to work. The team was made of real experts. Prof Graham Turner, an experienced researcher in sign language and sign language interpreting, managed the project and kept things pointing in the right direction. Tessa Slaughter is an experienced sign language interpreter who dealt with day-to-day organisation and offered valuable mentoring to the interpreters. I pulled together coaching resources and helped the interpreters build up their technical skills. The supervision of the interpreters was carried out by the team member whose work I want to discuss here: Dr Jules Dickinson.

Her work involved helping interpreters to process the emotions that arise during their interpreting, build resilience and work on their ethical decision-making. There are some interpreters for whom those topics will immediately sound familiar and welcome. Medical interpreters might be aware of their need to build resilience to deal with the difficulties they might face from one day to the next. Court interpreters might think back to assignments when they had to make an ethical decision in a far shorter time than they might have liked.

Recently, conference interpreters have begun to think through those issues too. Among the misleading cries that "We're in the booth, so we don't have to make difficult decisions" and "Well, it's all technical and we're neutral, so it's fine," there have been some interpreters who have realised that the booth might shield sound, but it doesn't keep out humanity and real life. We might have our interpreting mediated by equipment, but that doesn't lessen the force of dealing with angry speakers, off-colour jokes or attempts to hold us responsible for problems in an attempt to deflect the blame.

All interpreting involves ethical decision-making, emotions and a need for resilience. If it didn't, then the (in)famous AIIC workload study (AIIC, 2001) wouldn't have found such a high rate of emotional burnout among their conference interpreter members. If interpreters didn't need support teams, then we would never encounter assignments after which we get home and are only fit for binge-watching Netflix or grabbing random food before falling into bed.

No matter where we interpret, no matter who we interpret for, no matter our language pairs, as interpreters and as humans, we all need to work on ways to work through the emotions that come with the job, build our resilience and make ethical decisions, especially where there is no clear-cut answer.

Interpreting is interpreting and interpreters are interpreters. If sign language interpreters can benefit from the skills and questions of a professional supervisor, so can conference interpreters and business interpreters and medical interpreters and court interpreters. So who's got your back?

Who is working with you on your resilience? Who can you honestly share your emotions with and learn from? Who is digging under the surface of how you feel about that interpreting assignment that still sticks in your mind to this day? When was the last time you reflected on your interpreting practice with the help of someone else?

Interpreting has the strange distinction of being a social profession that can still create feelings of loneliness. Conference interpreters can spend all day in a small soundproof booth with a fellow interpreter and then head home, not knowing if anyone can really understand their feelings towards the clients, their fellow interpreters and even themselves. For those of us blessed with the opportunity to travel for assignments, the journey home can be both a welcome relief and a challenge.

In other interpreting settings, for some unfathomable reason, it is deemed fine for interpreters to work assignments on their own, no matter their length. Apparently, the XXth World Conference on Esoteric Llama Bathing absolutely must have two interpreters per language pair, but a murder trial or day of trauma counselling sessions only needs one. Interpreters who regularly work on their own certainly need some way of reflecting on their own practice and developing resilience.

If interpreting is to survive and thrive in the age of speech translation, then interpreters have to survive too. There's simply no point in pushing for the growth of a profession that loses people to emotional burnout at appalling rates (Nimdzi, 2019). Whatever we do to develop our skills, improve interpreting PR and market our services, we need systems and structures that will allow us to keep on delivering more than words for years to come.

I firmly believe that clinical supervision or something akin to it will play a vital role in the future of interpreting. Sure, when we are starting out, we might look for mentors and then we might invest in business consulting, but doing all that at the expense of building resilience and learning to consistently make ethical decisions well would be an example of professional myopia.

What are the realistic alternatives? There are none. At the end of an episode of the Troublesome Terps podcast, Justine Mason, a lecturer in mental health nursing, reflected on the need for emotional and mental health support for interpreters, with the words, "If you don't, you're gonna run out."[1] If we don't build our own support networks and at least look at clinical supervision, we're going to run out of resources to cope and one day, we will become yet another example of an interpreter who had to go through emotional burnout. If we don't make providing support structures a priority in every association, agency and even among peers, we're going to run out of interpreters.

It's as brutally simple as that. Can human interpreters survive in an AI-dominated world? The answer to that question is complex and contains a lot of ifs and buts. Unless we do something about helping interpreters build resilience, deal with the emotions that come with our work and consistently grow in our ethical decision-making and ability to reflect on our work, the answer is simple: we won't survive, no matter what the technology can do.

Sure, interpreting as a profession might survive. It has been going for thousands of years without any real support structures. Universities are continuing to churn out newly qualified graduates every year. Without the right support structures and the right people committing to take interpreter emotional and mental health seriously, we will keep losing interpreters. Let's put it like this: interpreting might well keep on going, but if you want to keep going as an interpreter, looking for clinical supervision and some clear way of working on the areas mentioned in this chapter should be as high, if not higher, on your list of priorities as learning to do better marketing or PR.

It's at this point that the answer to the question becomes personal. The most pertinent question for each person reading this isn't "Can human interpreters survive?" but "Can *you* survive?" The answer to that question is closely linked to the need to seek and find the kind of support already mentioned and also to a part of interpreting that is becoming more popular. It's time to look at precisely this area now.

Keeping your skills sharp

Cast your mind back to 2017. I was almost certainly attending every business networking meeting within a ten-mile radius and spending far too much time on Facebook groups. In March of that year, just as several US states were dealing with heavy snowstorms, I received an email about an interpreting project called Interpretimebank – a project that represented a shift in interpreter attitudes and behaviour.

For as long as I could remember, practising interpreting skills had been a touchy subject, especially for experienced professionals. Certainly, early in my career, I frequently came across people rolling out clichés such as "If you weren't good enough, you wouldn't be here," "The more assignments you do, the better you get" and "If you're trained, you're fine."

While anyone who looks hard enough can still find those attitudes present today, times have changed. Work by brave researchers like Elisabet Tiselius (2013) has shown the need for us to practice our skills, outside of the booth. Practice groups and intensive practice sessions have popped up in several locations around Europe. Websites like SpeechPool and the European Commission Speech Repository have simplified the task of finding relevant speeches to practice with. Still, the most common way to practice was on your own.

Although I have to admit being pretty sceptical at first, the idea of Interpretimebank is to change all that. Built in 2014 but really taking off in the past couple of years, it provides a way for people to get feedback from fellow interpreters on their interpreting, in return for offering the same service to others. Instead of working with yourself for company, their aim is to build a community of mutually supporting interpreters.

It's a lofty goal that is built on some important realities. Since the most common reason for an interpreter being called is that the users can't understand each other's languages, relying on client feedback on the quality of our work is not always helpful. They will be pretty good at helping us understand how well we are doing at client service and helping them reach their goals, but they definitely can't check our accuracy or terminological correctness. Similarly, relying on the assessment of the interpreters we share an assignment with assumes that they have the brain space and willingness to be alert to our performance at a time when they really should be concentrating on theirs. Besides, there aren't very many ways to tell a fellow interpreter that they have a glaring weakness without suffering from professional awkwardness. Recovering from that when you could be working with the same person next week takes impressive resilience.

Yet all but the most arrogant of us will be aware of areas where we could improve our performance. Perhaps we would like to be even better at reformulation or we want to do better when dealing with speakers with strong accents. It could be that our consecutive notetaking needs work or simply that we want to perform better in a certain domain. My most recent assignment showed me just how much better I perform with some subjects compared to others.

The idea behind coaching, whether it comes in the form of seeking peer assessments of our performance or something more structured is that we develop best when we have others to help us. While the most common method of doing this is still to work on entire speeches, there are now enough resources to try a very different and perhaps more fruitful approach.

As we saw in Chapter 2, one of the long-standing assumptions of cognitive studies of interpreting is that our work is a multistage process and that we can learn important lessons by trying to tease apart each of these stages. In a book review, interpreting researcher Kilian Seeber called this a "deconstructive approach" (Seeber, 2016). It might be more helpful to go with the label "component skills approach" in this chapter.

A component skills approach to interpreter coaching would argue that any disfluencies or issues we find in an interpreter's performance are simply the symptoms of some cognitive or technical issue. It could be as simple as the sound quality temporarily dipping or as deep as a misreading of the direction or intention of the text. Seen through that lens, practising entire speeches gives us the data to work on to set more specific training drills to improve that single area before trying again.

Imagine a golfer who wants to improve their score. They could, conceivably, spend all their time travelling the world playing course after course. A good coach might well take them to each hole and ask them to aim a little to the left or change their grip slightly. A better coach, however, would perhaps walk round as they play one hole and then use their knowledge and expertise to suggest that they spend more time on the driving range or work on muscle conditioning or see a nutritionist. Working on your game as a whole is great but sportspeople have known for decades that improvement can come quicker by pulling your game apart and working on individual components at a time.

While we still don't know for sure what all the component skills needed by interpreters are, we do know enough to be able to isolate some and create drills for them. Books such as *Conference Interpreting* by Andrew Gillies and papers by scholars such as Djovcos and Djovcosova (2013) contain a wealth of useful exercises. In the case of Djovcos and Djovcosova, their exercises are actually repurposed from those that have been clinically proven in another field.

What might this type of interpreter coaching look like in practice? The model is fairly simple.

The first stage in coaching would be for interpreters to either find a practice buddy or to join a practice group. Everyone would commit to reading through available materials on practice exercises and making sure that they have a good idea of what some of the component skills of interpreting might be. Each interpreter would then sit down and create a list of areas where they think they would like to improve.

The next stage would be to go through a practice speech, one between five and ten minutes long. This gives a decent amount of data to play with without anyone getting to the point where their concentration would naturally wane.

Interpreters would then take turns critically evaluating each other's perfor-mance. The key would be to avoid pointless remarks like "It's not a screw; it's a threaded fitting" or "You got the wrong conjugation of that verb." Remarks on isolated mistakes like those are rarely, if at all, useful for developing performance. Instead, the most helpful way is to look for trends in performance. Does the inter-preter seem to have trouble when they can't immediately find the right term? Is their vocal quality or intonation lacking in places? Do they sound hesitant?

From these trends, it would then be possible to build up a picture of the areas that need the most immediate attention alongside the areas noted down before doing the speech. For example, if an interpreter really struggles when they can't find terms offhand, some of the verbal fluency exercises created by Djovcos and Djovcosova (2013) will be useful. If they seem to have trouble with finding ways to summarise when necessary, there are exercises created by Andrew Gillies (2013) that can help.

It's important to reiterate that the point of coaching is not to collect errors or disfluencies but instead to look for patterns and try to find the underlying issue behind them. In my own practice, I have realised that I often interpret texts where the quality of presentation really matters. The audience needs to feel the emotion of the speaker or appreciate the artfulness of their speech. That means that I need to work hard on my public speaking skills in both English and French – my native and working language, respectively. This also means storing a bank of standard phrases for different types of events in both languages. I need to know immedi-ately how a French speaker might politely express disbelief or how a Scottish fisherman might expect to hear someone query a detail.

There are, of course, some global skills that apply to all interpreters. We can no longer keep on getting grumpy at the frequency of people using their second, third or fourth languages to speak at a conference. Sure, it isn't ideal, but it's not going to go away. This puts the onus on us as interpreters to practice interpreting speeches by non-native speakers and those with strong accents for other reasons.

Similarly, whether you work in courts or in schools, the likelihood is that you will have assignments that require you to shift registers. Speakers can and do pass from highly technical content to friendly chatter and back again within the space of a minute. Sometimes, for the sake of comprehension, the interpreter will need to summarise a highly specialised report into language that can be understood by someone who left school at the age of eight.

For interpreters who are looking to find places to start their development, look-ing back at recent assignments and noting down trends is ideal. Here's a very simple example from a recent assignment I did. I have anonymised the details.

Assignment:	Consultation to draft worldwide statement on dealing with XXXXX
Audience:	Senior leaders dealing with the issue every day.
Main difficulties:	Use of three different interpreting modes every day, content moving quickly from personal/emotional to technical, lots of specialist terminology.
Areas for development:	Working on French public speaking skills to keep the artistry and emotional impact of speeches, making self-corrections smoother, improving interrupting speakers so I can interpret, emotional resilience.

Notice how the areas for development span skills that are covered by both coaching and supervision. This is perfectly normal. Sometimes patterns that seem to point to technical issues such as chunking or verbal fluency are actually symptoms of the interpreter being tired or emotionally spent. Likewise, having a strong store of technical skills might give us the extra lift we need to carry on during emotionally difficult talks.

The idea behind coaching is for the coach and the person they coach to take ownership of their part of the process. There is no point in saying you will coach someone if all you're going to say is "Go interpret stuff" or "You need to practice your genitives." Likewise, there's no point in asking someone to coach you if you're going to get offended when they point out that maybe, just maybe, you need to practice putting more intonation into your interpreting or standing back further from the exact words being said.

Flexibility, vulnerability and determination to grow will always be the hallmark of people who keep on improving. With a horde of technologists trying to nip at our heels and produce gadgets and apps that, while not delivering perfect interpreting, do deliver something that sounds like it to the untrained ear, we really don't have much choice but to keep improving.

When we realise that we could do with a boost in a couple of technical areas, to take them from good enough to pass exams to good enough to wow clients, we need to get coaching. Until someone creates a specialist interpreter coaching course, that coaching will likely come from our peers, the very peers we work beside at events. Being brave enough to seek coaching and develop together, with no ego-clashes or shame, is a big ask of any interpreter. Being proud enough that we ignore our need to improve and thereby get left behind ultimately costs a lot more.

Building a coaching-supervision combo

Anyone who has played computer games will know about the importance of learning combos. These are special abilities you get by putting two or more moves together. In a football game, hitting just the right combo might mean that you can turn around quickly and sprint away from defenders. In fighting games, a quick combo can decide the result of your match. Even in chess, a combination of two or more tactics – like a fork and a pin – can win you pieces or end the game.

To ensure that humans stay ahead of the machines when it comes to interpreting, building a supervision-coaching combo could be a game changer. Personally, I know many interpreters who are keen on supervision but don't really get the need for coaching. Conversely, while the rise in practice groups among conference interpreters is fantastic, there hasn't been a corresponding growth in supervision.

When we realise that interpreters are emotional beings who need supervision to learn to process their emotions and build resilience as much as they are professionals who provide an added value service – and so need coaching – the need for combo-building becomes clear. If you are a conference interpreter, please never be tempted to think that clinical supervision is just for other interpreters. If you work all day in a school or medical centre, please don't imagine that coaching isn't for you.

The combo on the road

Some of the biggest learning moments for me over the past two or three years have come while leading workshops on Strategic CPD in a few locations in Europe for very different groups of translators and interpreters. For a while, it was my most-requested workshop, despite (or perhaps because of!) the fact that it is the workshop where I do very little talking.

Almost all of the workshop consists of my asking attendees to interview each other as to where they currently are in their interpreting, where they want to be and the areas where they feel they need to improve. It's hardly groundbreaking stuff, but I do encourage the people doing the interviews to refuse to be satisfied with the first answers they get. Instead, I ask them to probe deeper, asking lots of "why" questions and checking that they have understood correctly.

More often than not, the answers that come are focused on the same three areas: getting more work, delivering better work and building confidence. The last two of those areas happen to be two areas where supervision and coaching can really deliver. How much more confident would you be if you had developed the tools to be resilient in the face of angry, unrealistic clients, unclear speeches and emotional content? How much better could your work be if you were able to identify and improve the precise areas of your performance that are currently holding you back?

I have to admit that in some of those workshops I have been confronted with my own training and development needs. There's something very humbling about hearing people openly discuss the very areas where you need to grow but haven't yet asked someone to help. There is something very encouraging about hearing people with three times more experience than you express their desire to keep pushing the boundaries of what they could be capable of achieving.

Bringing it home

It's all very well thinking hard during workshops, but real growth is what happens when no one is looking. The interpreters who will continue to stay so far ahead of the machines that they never need to worry about them are those who put in the hard hours that never show up on Instagram or appear in magazines. Doing verbal fluency exercises in the shower, taking notes on public speaking skills and practicing them in your bedroom, using flights to think through your values and goals – that's when the changes come.

Anyone can talk or write a good game. Anyone with a smartphone can take a picture that makes them look successful. In my experience, some of the best interpreters are rarely found on Twitter or seen on Instagram. They're the ones you can depend on to pass you superb relay, deliver assignments under tough conditions and whose term lists make your work much easier.

What are you doing in-between assignments, in those hours when you could slack off or tune up your skills and no one but you would know the difference? We need to strike a balance between work and rest, but I have to admire those interpreters who pay, from their own money, to attend training courses or spend time in practice groups. I also admire those unseen interpreters who obviously keep their skills sharp. Every consultant keeps a list of the people they can rely on to deliver when it counts. We very quickly get to know the people who are determined to be the best they can be and those who try to get by with the minimum.

It's amazing how often clients can see the difference too. When you are networking and you manage to honestly say, "It's funny you should talk about selling widgets to ABCD Ltd, because I was using their CEO's last speech on YouTube to practice my interpreting," you will automatically have an advantage over the people who just want to send a quote out and move on to the next person. Even during an assignment, interpreters who are keen enough to chat with clients during lunch will always make a better impression than those who hide out in the booth.

While we normally measure how good an interpreter is by how they perform in the booth or on assignment, perhaps we need to challenge ourselves to be great interpreters at home, too. This might mean having the emotional resilience to realise that we don't need to win every assignment and that our rates need to be high enough to pay for time off to work on our skills and take supervision. It might mean being humble enough to approach a peer about doing some mutual coaching so we grow our skills together. It might be as simple as buying a book or reading an article with some practice exercises in it and committing to doing something about our interpreting a few days a week.

Surviving or thriving in the age of AI?

Throughout this book, a key theme has been the need to create ways for human interpreters to survive, given the march of speech translation. We've looked at how we got to this precarious-seeming position, what the future might hold and how we might get to a future where human interpreting is the gold standard. Recently, I was discussing this book with a colleague who felt compelled to correct me. "We shouldn't try to survive," he said. "What about thriving?"

He was right. While the PR machine of the big tech companies has set its sights on making it seem like our days are nearly over, we know better. We know that there is more than a small niche available to human interpreters. If we get this right, the growth in automated speech translation might actually become an opportunity for us. If the world ever gets access to accurate interpreting from machines, there might suddenly be greater awareness that accuracy is not nearly enough. My motto used to be "When I started out, I thought interpreting was language skills with people attached; now I realise it's people skills with language attached." Once we get ahold of that truth and our clients get ahold of that truth, the prospect of machines taking our jobs will be seen as pretty laughable, unless they can take our humanity too.

It's at that point that the content of this chapter and indeed the content of the last four chapters comes into its own. Any of us who were privileged enough to be trained in interpreting can be sure that we have the skills to deliver accuracy. We know that we understand both languages well enough to be able to comprehend what is being said and reformulate it in another language.

Back in Chapter 1, I told the story of the meeting that turned on the meaning of a single word. The chief executive I mentioned, who spoke French but now realised the power of interpreting, is a great example of how clients can learn to appreciate interpreters. He told me that he understood everything that was being said but not what was going on. He learned and I learned that day that there is a yawning gap between understanding a language and being able to understand what the language is doing.

Interpreters work in precisely that gap. The best machine can only ever use fancy mathematics to come up with a translation based on how words have been used before. No one is trying to get computers to understand that when the chair says *this*, it really means that they are looking for more information or when the doctor asks *that* question, what they're really looking for is an answer to help them with *that* part of the diagnostic process. Woe betide the interpreter who thinks that their job involves "just what the speaker said." We might say that we expect interpreters to produce idiomatic, natural-sounding language, but it's all too easy to forget that doing that well implies that we understand what kind of language fits that description in the very specific situations we find ourselves in.

We could all stand up and give lectures on cultural differences and how questions are asked or arguments developed in different cultures. While no two interpreters will agree on exactly how much we should adjust our output according to cultural expectations – the answer is most likely that it depends on context – what we do all agree on is that we use that knowledge in our work. If we are going to use that knowledge and employ a variety of techniques in our work, then that automatically means that we need to keep developing our techniques and increasing our knowledge so we can keep working more effectively.

In fact, this really takes us back to the conduit and triadic models of interpreting from Chapter 2. The more machines manage to do something close to the conduit model of interpreting, the more opportunities we have to explain why that doesn't work. While we've all been worrying whether we'd have a job in five years, all the hard work we have been doing with the aim of survival has positioned us to thrive. The very skills of effective PR, targeted marketing, expert delivery and ongoing professional development that we have been working on can carry us far beyond the point of survival.

Yes, it is true that some sections of interpreting continue to struggle, and we need to work together to get through that. Yes, it is also true that there are some clients who would prefer that interpreting was fast, cheap and practically invisible. Yes, it is true that the technology PR machine isn't going away.

While all of that is true, every professional interpreter I have ever met has the potential to use those challenges as springboards rather than obstacles. We can use dodgy technology PR as inspiration to change the way the world sees our work. We can use lowballing clients as inspirations to find and encourage better ones. We can work with interpreters in struggling sectors to get them more respect and a better deal.

I would hope that, by this stage, none of that seems theoretical or vague. Each sector has its own challenges and opportunities. While each country has its own economic imperative, the same principles apply wherever we live and whoever we work for. Wherever there is a genuine need for interpreters, the interpreters who do best are those who aren't afraid to look for new opportunities, refuse to be constrained by typical ways of working and are committed to doing their bit to improve the lot of their fellow interpreters. They go to tradeshows and events, network, do regular continued professional development, market themselves as businesses and not as wannabe employees, negotiate on an equal footing with agencies and learn how to walk away from the unreasonable ones and aren't afraid to win their own clients, when that is possible.

What is the future of human interpreters, given the rise of speech translation? That really depends on the interpreters.

Note

1   https://www.troubleterps.com/17

References

AIIC. 2001, *Interpreter workload study – full report, aiic.net.* <//aiic.net/page/657>.
Dean, R. K., Pollard, R. Q., Jr and English, M. A. 2004, 'Observation-supervision in mental health interpreter training', in *CIT: still shining after 25 years: proceedings of the 15th national convention of the conference of interpreter trainers*, CIT, Monmouth,

OR, pp. 55–75. <http://aladinrc.wrlc.org/bitstream/handle/1961/10196/CIT2004.pdf? sequence=1#page=62>.

Dean, R. K. and Pollard, R. Q. 2009, *I don't think we're supposed to be talking about this": case conferencing and supervision for interpreters. VIEWS.* <http://www.avlic.ca/sites /default/files/docs/AVLICNewsS-F2013DeanPollardArticle.pdf>.

Djovcos, M. and Djovcosova, Z. 2013, 'Aphasia and interpreting: aphasia-based interpreting exercises', *FORUM*, vol. 11, no. 1, pp. 23–49.

Gillies, A. 2013, *Conference interpreting: a student's practice book.* Routledge, Milton Park, Abingdon, Oxon.

Hetherington, A. 2012, 'Supervision and the interpreting profession: support and accountability through reflective practice', *International Journal of Interpreter Education*, vol. 4, no. 1, pp. 46–57.

Nimdzi (2019), 'The cost of caring', <https://www.nimdzi.com/the-cost-of-caring-vic arious-trauma-in-interpreters/>

Seeber, K. 2016, *Review of: conference interpreting: a complete course by R. Setton and A. Dawrant, aiic.net.* <//aiic.net/page/7798>.

Tiselius, E. 2013, *Experience and expertise in conference interpreting: an investigation of swedish conference interpreters*, University of Bergen.

Level 5

One last thought

That's how it all ends. With the right PR, marketing, value and team-work, human interpreters will have careers forever. The speech transla-tion makers will be crowded into a low-value corner, no one will ever believe that technology can replace us and the world will be full of rain-bows and butterflies.

GAME OVER

Things in life are rarely that simple. Very few things in any part of inter-preting are ever that simple. However much we might want to paint tech-nology as the implacable enemy of all that is good about interpreting, it's going to be there, whether we like it or not. If we accept that, we will realise that we will need to adopt a stance that is less like Spartacus and more like the conductor of a symphony. Fighting against technology won't get us very far. Working with technology will.

You might have heard the quote from Bill Wood, founder of DS Interpretation. He once said: "Interpreters will not be replaced by technol-ogy; they will be replaced by interpreters who use technology." It's neat and easy to remember, but is it right?

There is just one more chapter left of this book. In it I will make a sug-gestion that will either sound like common sense or a dangerous dalliance, depending on how you think. The final part of winning the war against artificial intelligence, speech translation and the like is actually not to fight at all but to use all the technology that seems to be ranged against us to improve our own work and produce output that is of a higher quality than ever seen before. The final part of learning to survive interpreting in a high-tech world is to learn how to use that very world to our advantage.

Chapter 14

It's time to call a truce

The endings of many of my favourite childhood computer games were very similar. First off, there would be some kind of screen to show you that you had won, and then the triumphant music would start before a long scrolling list of the people who made the game. After a long process (and often two very sore thumbs), you had made it. The end of level baddies had been beaten, the trophy had been won, the special moves had been memorised. You had won.

And so we reach the end of this book. After spending all this time talking about how to show the world that human interpreting is the gold standard, after putting it all into practice, we can now relax and read the written equivalent of a victory screen. I can't quite give you any triumphant music but you have completed the task. Humans have won. It's over. Well done. As I said in **Level 5**:

GAME OVER

Or maybe not. Maybe we have been thinking the wrong way all along. It's obviously going to be important to combat the misstatements and borderline lies of the "machine interpreting" community. It will be vital to keep ourselves on the top of our game while generating the kind of PR that demonstrates our worth to society. But do we really need the conflict metaphor? Is our profession destined to be an ongoing rage against the machines? Are we forced into fighting for our corner against the technological giants?

As much as the world loves a good David and Goliath story of a plucky small kid downing the fearsome, over-equipped giant, that doesn't have to be the story of interpreting. For every big trend in interpreting, there are local exceptions, and every threat contains an opportunity within it.

The big trend in interpreting in many markets is that contracts are becoming bigger and more centralised, and where there are centralised contracts, there is cost-cutting. Where there is cost-cutting, there is an open door for speech translation to be an option. Yet for all the changes brought by the UK Government's central contract for all court and police interpreting, stories continue to roll in of local courts and local police stations bypassing central purchasing and going back to the tried and tested interpreters they know. For every agency taking what seems to be huge chunks of the market, there are tales of interpreters finding new business opportunities for clients who want a different service than agencies can provide.

With the threat of big contracts come opportunities for interpreters willing to learn and apply business skills. Could the threat of machine interpreting lead to something useful for the profession too?

Imagine yourself working in your normal interpreting environment but now you have a new gadget with you. This gadget listens in to the interpreting and picks up on any terminology that you haven't memorised. Within a fraction of a second, it tags the term, looks it up using the exact resources you would use, generates the most likely useful translation in the precise context you are in and prompts you with it, either visually or with audio.

That would be useful, wouldn't it? Any technology that can even get close to producing machine interpreting could easily produce that. In fact, in conversations with computing experts, I have been reliably informed that devices like that are within current technological limits. We already have decently reliable voice recognition in many languages, fast background searching has been around for a while and it would not be hard to teach computers your favourite resources and their priority. We are just waiting for someone to put those ideas together.

How about error checking? While I have responded sceptically about a recent system that Machine Translation experts have created to check for errors in interpreting (Bond, 2018), it is possible that, with the right nudging, a useful system could be created. Imagine having a device that would notify you when you have made a small error – getting a name wrong or forgetting a negation – and help you to correct it. Again, that might sound like science fiction but it is entirely within the realms of near future technology.

Smart interpreters could think of many use cases of current and near future technology. We already have paperless booths, terminology memorisation tools and the ability to check term bases on the fly. Why not imagine technology as giving us a way to offer even better quality rather than only seeing it as a risk?

None of this excuses the excesses of the speech translation industry and none of it should tempt us to lower our guard. We still cannot rest on our laurels and think that we will automatically be fine. But we can make technology our ally rather than our enemy.

For examples of how this might work, we just need to look around us. When I was a teenager, I used to play chess competitively. I grew up admiring the seemingly unstoppable attacking work of Garry Kasparov and the ability of Nigel Short to find a counter-attack in what looked like hopeless positions. When those two ruled the roost, playing chess on a computer was a good way to get a laugh. Unless you had amazing hardware and a seriously expensive chess engine, the likelihood was that anyone who knew a decent number of openings and the beginnings of attacking chess could get a good result.

That isn't the case anymore. About a year ago, I downloaded a Stockfish app onto my phone. At that point, it was the strongest chess engine on the planet. At anything other than the lowest level, my smartphone, which is about as heavy as a chocolate bar, defeated me soundly. In fact, Stockfish on a three-year-old smartphone can beat any professional chess player alive. Very recently, Google announced that they managed to build a chess system that started from nothing but the basic rules of chess and was good enough within three months to continually beat the newest version of Stockfish available on the fastest machine they could find.

Computers absolutely wreck humans at chess. Yet, despite that, there are still chess professionals. None of them complain that computers ruined their profession. Quite the contrary, they now train with the computers: analysing every game their opponents have played in the last year with a few clicks, training on specific tactics and openings while travelling, locating new ideas while they are packing.

Even in an area where machines have undeniably outclassed humans, humans are finding benefits from the machines being there. Rather than their being a threat, it turns out that machines actually improve human performance.

Of course, professional chess and professional interpreting are not exactly comparable. Chess is a game or a sport, and the attraction of watching chess for its fans is not in seeing the best chess possible but in seeing how humans do against each other. Interpreting, as this book has tried to emphasise, always exists for a purpose. If at any point, machines get better than humans at achieving that purpose, human professionals will likely be out of a job.

Whether you think that point is coming next month, next year or never depends a lot on what you think human interpreters do and what you think of the current state of the technology. No matter your answer, the point remains the same: seeing technology as an ally produces the best results.

Another example is in medicine. While the designers who created specialised learning systems such as IBM Watson claim that the systems can be used to suggest diagnoses that doctors haven't previously thought of, they still require human support to confirm these (Svenstrup, Jørgensen and Winther, 2015). In fact, recent checking has found that such systems just tell doctors what they already knew (Doctorow, 2017). At best, they support the work of doctors, rather than taking their jobs. You still need the people skills of a human being to move from diagnosis to persuading people to follow the right treatment for their condition. It's all well and good looking up your symptoms online but you still need someone to check out what you find and then help you through the stages until you are well.

Rather than taking human jobs, it seems that advances in technology are instead helping humans do better at their work, at least for the time being. It makes sense to actively search for places where human interpreters can use machines to their advantage. Interpreting in an AI world might just mean allowing machines to do some of the heavy lifting, leaving interpreters to put our brains to their best use.

This is not quite the same as what was discussed in the chapter on finding niches. Working with the machines doesn't mean that we sit back and only intervene in those rare moments where sarcasm or irony or cultural nuance mean that we have to take over. Quite the contrary, working with machines should mean that we perform better from the first moment we meet a potential client to the final "clink" of their payment into our bank accounts.

A machine-integrated interpreting workflow might look like this:

When we meet a potential client, we input their details into a Client Relationship Management system (with their permission, of course). That CRM tracks communication and reminds us to send them any info they asked for within the time they requested it. It also reminds us to check up on them periodically and mines publicly available information on them to suggest useful sales approaches. Useful information like upcoming conferences or mentions in industry press are sent to us as prompts for catch-up emails.

Once we have a sale, automated team-building software reads through the records of interpreters we have worked with to suggest the best people for the job or, if we are interpreting on our own, the same software pulls up related projects for us to learn from.

During the preparation phase, we work with two useful tools. We feed all the client documents into automated term miners, which extract terms that aren't in our database for us to check, while pulling together relevant existing terms. At the same time, preparation software suggests relevant articles for us to read and helpful practice materials.

As we work during the assignment, term alert apps listen in and pull new terminology for us, while flagging up terms that are already in the database. Performance trackers listen for signs of fatigue to remind us to take breaks or swap with a boothmate, if that is relevant.

Once the assignment is finished, automated invoicing and expense tracking software creates the invoice for us to send, while dietary management software looks through our recent health info and reads our vital signs to suggest the ideal foods to eat to aid recovery.

That all sounds like a work of science fiction but technophile readers will soon spot how many of those technologies are available in embryonic form today. With workflows like that, humans remain in the driving seat, while machines do all the laborious or finicky work that human brains weren't really designed for. I can't be the only interpreter whose attempts to help colleagues with terminology have been confounded due to slow typing and less-than-faultless Wi-Fi. We can and should do better.

While it will remain true that human interpreters will have to fight for their status and stand against the dubious and damaging claims of some unscrupulous PR and marketing from some parts of the technology industries, we must resist the temptation to become anti-technology holdouts. Rather than allowing technology to sweep us away or ignoring the incessant speech translation adverts, we need to make technology work for us, finding ways that it can be inserted into our practice to enable us to deliver better quality.

At this point, some readers will be thinking that I am heading towards that famous quote from Bill Wood that I mentioned earlier: "Interpreters will not be replaced by technology but by interpreters who know how to use technology."

That quote may sound rather clever, but it masks the complexities of the world we now live in.

There is a danger in technology becoming overhyped and under-thought. It cannot be the centre of our practice. Use of technology will not be the sole determining factor in the future of interpreters. Being clever about the business decisions we make will be.

The interpreter who, faced with the march of speech translation, decides to adopt every single app and every single gadget that could possibly have something to do with interpreting is not smart, but stupid. You can have all the accounting and expense apps you like but if you never get a project that requires them, you have wasted your money. An interpreter can build the world's sleekest CRM system but if they don't know how to build relationships in real-life, without the help of automated emailing systems, they will never get the best assignments or get to work with the nicest colleagues.

Technologies are tools; interpreters should be master craftspeople. A great sculptor is great even with a rusty old chisel. A truly great musician can make an average instrument sound like it belongs on the finest stage. A poor singer sounds like a poor singer no matter the quality of the sound system – I did live sound engineering and used to sing in a church for several years—I know that last one from painful personal experience!

All a tool can ever do is enhance the quality that an artist has. Automated term mining still relies on humans deciding which terms are worth noticing and how best to understand them. Smart systems for estimating quality and fatigue are only useful to interpreters who understand quality and fatigue already.

If all this is confusing, it doesn't have to be. We can and probably should simultaneously hold in our minds a commitment to making the best use of technological developments while championing the power and skill of human interpreters. It does not degrade our profession at all to admit that we can benefit from technology in the same way as many translators have benefitted in the growth of Computer Aided Translation. Yet the ongoing arguments over whether Computer Aided Translation tools have actually caused issues with the status of translators and how they are trained to treat texts (Pym, 2011) should act as a way of balancing out the tendency towards hype. Adopting tools has to be done for a reason and with possible unhelpful side effects in mind.

In interpreting, a perfect example can be found in video remote interpreting (VRI), a subject I had deliberately avoided writing about until now. I recently wrote a chapter of an e-book for the Institute of Translation and Interpreting,[1] in which I reviewed all the available evidence on VRI, from its use helping Deaf people who need to access core public services to its use in allowing multilingual webinars.

Across every use case of VRI, no matter the language or country, the effects seem to be the same. Yes, VRI does increase access to interpreting and allows multi-hub events. Yes, it perfectly meshes with new ways of presenting information, such as webinars. It has undeniable benefits, but it has undeniable problems, too.

Interpreters fatigue more quickly when using VRI. Quality, though seemingly comparable to in-person interpreting across some measures, drops more quickly than it does in person. Worse still, interpreters in almost every study reported difficulties in building rapport with the people they were interpreting for, a sense of being distant from proceedings, a lack of control and difficulty in using those interpersonal skills that they had worked so hard on – the very interpersonal skills that set human interpreters apart from machines.

VRI is therefore an incredibly useful tool, and it would be unhelpful to recommend that we entirely ignore the hard work of all the developers who have tried to perfect it. As useful as it is, its serious flaws mean that we have to use it carefully. It makes interpreting more accessible but to the likely detriment of interpreter well-being and our ability to use some of the key skills that set us apart from machines. This is why I was glad to see that same association publish a position paper on VRI outlining those precise advantages and disadvantages alongside specific guidance on how to deal with them.

A similar effect can be found in simultaneous consecutive interpreting – a new interpreting mode which sees interpreters take consecutive-style notes while recording the speech, before giving a simultaneous rendition using their notes and the recording once the speaker is finished. It sounds cool and shows some potential for increasing accuracy. Yet, in the few studies where it has been compared to more common interpreting modes (discussed in Orlando, 2014), it seems that there is a risk that interpreters using this mode concentrate too much on the technology and their notes and lose eye contact with the audience. It may just be that it is so new that we haven't learned how to use it properly, or it may be that technology overload will always reduce interpreter performance. No one knows for sure.

These are just two examples, but it would be easy enough to imagine similar effects with other technology. Could automated term mining increase our efficiency in finding new terminology at the cost of our forgetting how to skim and scan documents? Could automated quality checking make us too reliant on numerical measures of interpreting performance at the cost of the intuition that interpreters build up as they work regularly in a team with the same people?

The time is ripe for interpreters to adopt new technologies. We can find ways of turning attempts at speech translation to our advantage, but for our own good and for the good of our clients, we can't go into any of this blindly. We are professionals. A mark of professionalism is the ability and willingness to take the hard decisions, based on our current knowledge and experience so that we get the best results.

Very few people would have any respect for a doctor who decided that, since IBM Watson is getting good at some diagnoses, they could stop reading medical journals. There aren't many people who would excuse librarians for sitting in the back, drinking tea all day because you can now check the book catalogue online. If we wouldn't accept such lazy, apathetic behaviour from other professionals, we can't excuse it in ourselves.

Let's go back to the quote that I used earlier in this chapter.

> Interpreters will not be replaced by technology but by interpreters who know how to use technology.

After all this discussion of the need to adopt technology sensibly, is this quote still valid? When I wrote a post discussing this quote on my business blog,[2] it turned out that it really depends on how you read it. If you read it in the way I have read it and the way that some technology fans have used it, then it is clearly flawed. Often people see the quote as mandating that all interpreters jump on the technology bandwagon right now or be left behind.

Take, for example, one article where Hélène Pielmeyer from Common Sense Advisory argued that interpreters who didn't throw themselves headfirst into VRI would soon find themselves struggling for work (Pielmeyer, 2017). Going by their own research, which has consistently shown that technology providers of VRI in spoken languages have often struggled to find a market, this is patently absurd. It also relegates poor interpreters to being those who are simply swept away by market change, without any power to affect their own destinies.

The future doesn't belong to weak interpreters, tossed about by every wave of doctrine but to those who make smart decisions. Any interpreter who based their decisions on the whims of technology marketing people would end up bankrupt and confused within a few months.

If the idea of interpreters being replaced by those who use technology means that we have to let the new technologies lead, then we might as well sign over our lives to Google now. Interpreters who know how to use technology and so want to use it for every problem are the same as a mechanic who only ever learned to use a hammer and tried to use that to change a tire. Contrary to popular belief, there isn't always "an app for that."

Some problems need fancy technical solutions; some need human thinking; some need both. When it comes to the future of interpreting, it is doubtful that technology use alone will determine anything. Remember, all a tool can do is simply add on to the skill that is already there. For every story of cars making buggy whip manufacturers extinct and iPhones all but wiping out Blackberry handsets, there are tales of gyrocopters failing to take off (if you'll pardon the pun) and nuclear trains failing to start a chain reaction.

Others, however, have read the pithy quote as suggesting that the future will belong to interpreters who make the best use of tools. That suggestion just might get us somewhere. Being smart with tools means knowing not just how to use them but when and why. A very good consultant interpreter should know instinctively when VRI is a good idea and when the clients need expert interpreters in the room. Similarly, a good business interpreter should know when everyone will benefit from their breaking out the simultaneous consecutive equipment and when they can leave it at home.

The same general rule works across every form of interpreting. When interpreters really understand the technology available and know the requirements of their clients well enough, they can make the right decision for each individual case. The great interpreter of the future will not just be amazingly accurate and pleasant to listen to, they will be a fully fledged consultant, knowing exactly which technologies work best for each individual use case and each individual client. The days of one-size-fits-all are slowly coming to an end. Long live the flexible-minded interpreter.

If this seems like a big ask, it's because it is. No one ever said that the future of interpreting would be easy. No one has ever claimed that surviving in the age of speech translation will be straightforward. If anything, the rise of artificial intelligence and high-tech solutions should serve as a prompt to push human intelligence further. The better speech translation gets, the better we need to get.

How do we even begin? Even this book has just scratched the surface, and all the techniques that were state-of-the-art when I wrote this will almost certainly be yesterday's news by the time you get to read it. We have long passed the point where any one person could know everything that would be useful for their business.

We can't know everything there is to know or master every tool, but we can work together. There are some interpreters, like my Troublesome Terps co-host Alexander Drechsel, who are walking tablet- and app-encyclopedias. Others, like Prof Barry Olsen and Ewandro Magalhaes, know VRI platforms better than anyone else on the planet. Still others, like Prof Kilian Seeber, are researchers in how interpreters' brains work. Around the world, there are expert interpreters on every area of the business and every technology we need to know about.

Maybe interpreters won't be replaced by technology nor by interpreters who know technology. Perhaps, the truth is that the interpreters who do well from now on will be those who know enough experts in enough areas to make excellent business, technology and self-development decisions. After all, interpreters don't exist to serve technology companies or to act as "resources" for large agencies. The point of interpreters is to provide excellent service to clients by enabling them to talk to people they could never have talked to without us.

Interpreting makes a difference. Interpreting in an AI age won't change that; it will simply enable us to make even more of a difference if and only if we are prepared to continually learn, grow and deliver added value to clients, using whichever technologies are appropriate. In an age of growing artificial intelligence, it is down to human intelligence to deliver when it really matters. Are you ready for that kind of excellent interpreting?

Notes

1 You can download it here: https://www.iti.org.uk/more/news/249-downloads/121
   6-new-research-initiative.
2 https://www.integritylanguages.co.uk/2018/07/13/replacing-interpreters-with-inte
   rpreters-who-know-technology/.

References

Bond, E. 2018, *Simultaneous interpreters may soon get real-time help just when they need it, slator*. <https://slator.com/academia/simultaneous-interpreters-may-soon-get-real-time-help-just-when-they-need-it/>.

Doctorow, C. 2017, *Watson for oncology isn't an AI that fights cancer, it's an unproven mechanical turk that represents the guesses of a small group of doctors, Boing Boing.* <https://boingboing.net/2017/11/13/little-man-behind-the-curtain.html>.

Orlando, M. 2014, 'A study on the amenability of digital pen technology in a hybrid mode of interpreting: consec-simul with notes', *Translation & Interpreting*, vol. 6, no. 2, pp. 39–54.

Pielmeyer, H. 2017, 'Interpreting delivery platforms: should you get on the bandwagon?' *ATA interpreters division*, 28 February. <http://www.ata-divisions.org/ID/interpreting-delivery-platforms-get-bandwagon/>

Pym, A. 2011, 'What technology does to translating', *Translation & Interpreting*, vol. 3, no. 1, pp. 1–9.

Svenstrup, D., Jørgensen, H. L. and Winther, O. 2015, 'Rare disease diagnosis: a review of web search, social media and large-scale data-mining approaches', *Rare Diseases*, vol. 3, no. 1, p. e1083145.

Bibliography

AIIC. 1999, 'Practical guide for conference interpreters', *aiic.net*. <http://aiic.net/p/628>.

AIIC. 2001, *Interpreter workload study – full report, aiic.net*. <//aiic.net/page/657>.

AIIC. 2004, *Conference interpreting is the interpretation of a conference, aiic.net*. <//aiic. net/page/4003>.

AIIC. 2016, *AIIC–Let Them Hear YOU (Eng): the added value of professional interpreters, YouTube*. <https://www.youtube.com/watch?v=7E_tQAsep7Y>.

Angelelli, C. 2004a, *Medical interpreting and cross-cultural communication*, Cambridge University Press.

Angelelli, C. 2004b, *Revisiting the interpreter's role: a study of conference, court, and medical interpreters in Canada, Mexico, and the United States*, John Benjamins Publishing Company, Amsterdam.

Angermeyer, P. S. 2015, *Speak English or what?: Codeswitching and interpreter use in New York City Courts*, Oxford University Press.

Beaton, M. 2007a, 'Interpreted ideologies in institutional discourse: the case of the European Parliament', *The Translator*, vol. 13, no. 2, pp. 271–96.

Beaton, M. 2007b, *Intertextuality and ideology in interpreter-mediated communication : the case of the European Parliament*, Unpublished PhD Thesis, Heriot-Watt University. <http://www.ros.hw.ac.uk/handle/10399/2028>.

Berk-Seligson, S. 2002, *The bilingual courtroom: court interpreters in the judicial process*, University of Chicago Press, Chicago, IL.

Best, J. 2013, *IBM Watson: the inside story of how the Jeopardy-winning supercomputer was born, and what it wants to do next, TechRepublic*. <https://www.techrepublic.com/ article/ibm-watson-the-inside-story-of-how-the-jeopardy-winning-supercomputer-was -born-and-what-it-wants-to-do-next/>.

Bond, E. 2018, *Simultaneous interpreters may soon get real-time help just when they need it, slator*. <https://slator.com/academia/simultaneous-interpreters-may-soon-get-rea l-time-help-just-when-they-need-it/>.

Braun, S. 2013, 'Keep your distance? Remote interpreting in legal proceedings: a critical assessment of a growing practice1', *Interpreting*, vol. 15, no. 2, pp. 200–28. doi:10.1075/intp.15.2.03bra.

Braun, S. and Taylor, J. 2012, 'Video-mediated interpreting: an overview of current practice and research', in Braun, S. and Taylor, J. (eds.), *Video conference and remote interpreting in criminal proceedings*, Intersential, Antwerp, pp. 33–68.

Bühler, H. 1985, 'Conference interpreting: a multichannel communication phenomenon', *Meta*, vol. 30, no. 1, pp. 49–54.

Chernov, G. V. 1979, 'Semantic aspects of psycholinguistic research in simultaneous interpretation', *Language and speech*, vol. 22, no. 3, pp. 277–95.

Christoffels, I. K., De Groot, A. M. and Waldorp, L. J. 2003, 'Basic skills in a complex task: a graphical model relating memory and lexical retrieval to simultaneous interpreting', *Bilingualism: Language and Cognition*, vol. 6, no. 3, pp. 201–11.

Clifford, A. 2004, 'Is fidelity ethical? The social role of the healthcare interpreter', *TTR: Traduction, Terminologie, Rédaction*, vol. 17, no. 2. <http://www.erudit.org/revue/tt r/2004/v17/n2/013273ar.html>.

Darò, V. 1989, 'The role of memory and attention in simultaneous interpretation: a neurolinguistic approach', *The Interpreter's Newsletter*, vol. 2, pp. 50–6.

Dean, R. K. 2014, 'Condemned to repetition? An analysis of problem-setting and problem-solving in sign language interpreting ethics', *Translation & Interpreting*, vol. 6, no. 1, pp. 60–75.

Dean, R. K. and Pollard, R. Q. 2001, 'Application of demand-control theory to sign language interpreting: implications for stress and interpreter training', *Journal of Deaf Studies and Deaf Education*, vol. 6, no. 1, pp. 1–14.

Dean, R. K. and Pollard, R. Q. 2004, 'A practice-profession model of ethical reasoning', *Views*, vol. 21, no. 9, p. 1.

Dean, R. K. and Pollard, R. Q. 2006, 'From best practice to best practice process: shifting ethical thinking and teaching', in *A new chapter in interpreter education: accreditation, research and technology: proceedings of the 16th national convention of the conference of interpreter trainers*, Monmouth, OR: CIT, pp. 119–32. <http://doc.wrlc.org/bitst ream/handle/1961/10197/CIT2006.pdf?sequence=3#page=127>.

Dean, R. K. and Pollard, R. Q. 2009, *I don't think we're supposed to be talking about this": case conferencing and supervision for interpreters*, VIEWS. <http://www.avlic.ca/sites /default/files/docs/AVLICNewsS-F2013DeanPollardArticle.pdf>.

Dean, R. K., Pollard, R. Q., Jr and English, M. A. 2004, 'Observation-supervision in mental health interpreter training', in *CIT: still shining after 25 years: proceedings of the 15th national convention of the conference of interpreter trainers*, CIT, Monmouth, OR, pp. 55–75. <http://aladinrc.wrlc.org/bitstream/handle/1961/10196/CIT2004.pdf? sequence=1#page=62>.

Dillinger, M. 1994, 'Comprehension during interpreting: what do interpreters know that bilinguals don't', in Lambert, S. and Moser-Mercer, B. (eds.), *Bridging the gap: empirical research in simultaneous interpretation*, John Benjamins, Amsterdam, pp. 155–89.

Diriker, E. 2004, *De-/re-contextualizing conference interpreting: interpreters in the ivory tower?* John Benjamins Publishing Company, Amsterdam.

Diriker, E. 2011, 'Agency in conference interpreting: still a myth?', *Gramma: Journal of Theory and Criticism*, vol. 19, pp. 27–36.

Djovcos, M. and Djovcosova, Z. 2013, 'Aphasia and Interpreting: aphasia-based interpreting exercises', *FORUM*, vol. 11, no. 1, pp. 23–49.

Doctorow, C. 2017, *Watson for oncology isn't an AI that fights cancer, it's an unproven mechanical turk that represents the guesses of a small group of doctors*, Boing Boing. <https://boingboing.net/2017/11/13/little-man-behind-the-curtain.html>.

Downie, J. 2009, *The end of an era: does Skopos theory spell the end of the 'free vs. literal' paradigm? Pneuma review: In depth* (Online). <http://www.academia.edu/d ownload/30862247/JDownie-EndOfAnEra.pdf>.

Downie, J. 2015, 'What every client wants? (Re) mapping the trajectory of client expectations research', *Meta: Journal des traducteurs/Meta:Translators' Journal*, vol. 60, no. 1, pp. 18–35.

Downie, J. 2017, 'Finding and critiquing the Invisible interpreter – a response to Uldis Ozolins', *Interpreting*, vol. 19, no. 2, pp. 260–70.

Downie, J. 2019, *Confex and the future of international events, integrity languages*. <https://www.integritylanguages.co.uk/2019/04/11/confex-and-the-future-of-international-events/>.

Dutoit, T. 2013, *An introduction to text-to-speech synthesis*, Springer Science & Business Media.

Eraslan, S. 2011, *International knowledge transfer in Turkey: the consecutive interpreter's role in context*, Unpublished PhD Thesis, Rovira i Virgili University.

Fiederer, R. and O'Brien, S. 2009, 'Quality and machine translation: a realistic objective?', *The Journal of Specialised Translation*, no. 11, pp. 52–74.

Gao, W. 2011, *Coherence in simultaneous interpreting: an idealized cognitive model perspective*, Thesis, Heriot-Watt University. <https://www.ros.hw.ac.uk/handle/10399/2504>.

Gerver, D. 1971, 'Simultaneous and consecutive interpretation and human information processing.'<http://www.eric.ed.gov/ERICWebPortal/recordDetail?accno=ED084906>.

Gile, D. 1990, 'L'évaluation de la qualité de l'interprétation par les délégués: une étude de cas', *The Interpreters' Newsletter*, vol. 3, pp. 66–71.

Gile, D. 1990, 'Scientific research vs. personal theories in the investigation of interpretation', in Gran, L. and Taylor, C. (eds.), *Aspects of applied and experimental research on conference interpretation*, Campanotto Editore, Udine, pp. 28–41.

Gile, D. 1991, 'The processing capacity issue in conference interpretation', *Babel*, vol. 37, no. 1, pp. 15–27.

Gile, D. 1995, *Basic concepts and models for interpreter and translator training*, J. Benjamins Publishing Company.

Gile, D. 1999, 'Testing the Effort Models' tightrope hypothesis in simultaneous interpreting-A contribution', *Hermes*, vol. 23, no. 1999, pp. 153–72.

Gile, D. 2001, 'Consecutive vs. Simultaneous: which is more accurate?', *The Journal of the Japan Association for Interpretation Studies*, vol. 1, pp. 8–20.

Gile, D. 2009, *Basic concepts and models for interpreter and translator training*, John Benjamins Publishing Company, Amsterdam.

Gillies, A. 2013, *Conference interpreting: a student's practice book*, Routledge, Milton Park, Abingdon, Oxon.

Google. 2017, *Google Pixel Buds—wireless headphones that help you do more*, Google. <https://www.blog.google/products/pixel/pixel-buds/>.

Hatim, B. and Mason, I. 1997, *The translator as communicator*, Routledge.

Hervais-Adelman, A. G., Moser-Mercer, B. and Golestani, N. 2011, 'Executive control of language in the bilingual brain: integrating the evidence from neuroimaging to neuropsychology', *Frontiers in psychology*, vol. 2, p. 234.

Hetherington, A. 2012, 'Supervision and the interpreting profession: support and accountability through reflective practice', *International Journal of Interpreter Education*, vol. 4, no. 1, pp. 46–57.

Google AI Blog. no date, 'How Google Translate squeezes deep learning onto a phone', *Google AI Blog*, <http://ai.googleblog.com/2015/07/how-google-translate-squeezes-deep.html>.

TEDEd. 2016, *How interpreters juggle two languages at once*, TEDEd. <https://ed.ted. com/lessons/how-interpreters-juggle-two-languages-at-once-ewandro-magalhaes>.

AIIC. 2012, *Interpretation is spoken, translation is written, aiic.net*. <//aiic.net/page/4002>.

Waverly Labs. 2017, 'Interview with Nicholas Ruiz on speech translation', *Waverly Labs*, 14 June. <https://web.archive.org/web/20170801011511/http://www.waverlylabs.com/ 2017/06/speech_translation_interview>.

Isham, W. P. 1994, 'Memory for sentence form after simultaneous interpretation: Evidence both for and against deverbalization', in Lambert, S. and Moser-Mercer, B. (eds.), *Bridging the gap: empirical research in simultaneous interpretation*, John Benjamins: Amsterdam, pp. 191–211.

Karlik, J. 2010, 'Interpreter-mediated scriptures: expectation and performance', *Interpreting*, vol. 12, no. 2, pp. 160–85. doi:10.1075/intp.12.2.03kar.

Koehn, P. et al. 2007, 'Moses: open source toolkit for statistical machine translation', in *Proceedings of the 45th annual meeting of the ACL on interactive poster and demonstration sessions*, Association for Computational Linguistics, pp. 177–80.

Koehn, P. 2009, *Statistical machine translation*, Cambridge University Press.

Koehn, P. 2017, 'Neural machine translation', *arXiv Preprint*. <http://arxiv.org/ abs/1709.07809>.

Kohn, K. and Kalina, S. 1996, 'The strategic dimension of interpreting', *Meta: Journal des traducteurs/Meta: Translators' Journal*, vol. 41, no. 1, pp. 118–38.

Läubli, S., Sennrich, R. and Volk, M. 2018, 'Has machine translation achieved human parity? A case for document-level evaluation', *arXiv preprint arXiv:1808.07048*.

Lederer, M. 1997, 'La théorie interprétative de la traduction: un résumé', *Revue des lettres et de traduction*, no. 3, 1997, 11–20.

Lemetty, S. 1999, *Review of speech synthesis technology*, MTech Thesis. Helsinki University of Technology. <http://research.spa.aalto.fi/publications/theses/lemmet ty_mst/index.html>.

Leprince-Ringuet, D. 2018, 'Why is Google's live translation so bad? We asked some experts', *Wired UK*, 22 October. <https://www.wired.co.uk/article/live-translation-p ixel-buds>.

Macchi, M. 1998, 'Issues in text-to-speech synthesis', in *Proceedings IEEE International Joint Symposia on Intelligence and Systems, 1998*. IEEE, pp. 318–25.

Mason, I. (ed.) 2001, *Triadic exchanges: studies in dialogue interpreting*, St. Jerome, Manchester.

Matthews, J. 2006, 'Review of: Ebru Diriker (2004). *De-/re-contextualizing conference interpreting: interpreters in the ivory tower?*', *JoSTrans: Journal of Specialized Translation*, vol. 5, pp. 151–7.

Moser-Mercer, B. 2002, 'Process models in simultaneous interpretation', in Pochhacker, F. and Shlesinger, M. (eds.), *The interpreting studies reader*, Routledge, London, pp. 149–61.

Napier, J. 2004, 'Interpreting omissions: a new perspective', *Interpreting*, vol. 6, no. 2, pp. 117–42.

Napier, J. and Barker, R. 2004, 'Sign language interpreting: the relationship between metalinguistic awareness and the production of interpreting omissions', *Sign Language Studies*, vol. 4, no. 4, pp. 369–93.

Och, F. J. 2002, *Statistical machine translation: from single-word models to alignment templates*, PhD Thesis, Bibliothek der RWTH Aachen.

Olsen, B. 2019, *Watch how interpreters do their jobs | WIRED video | CNE*. <https://video.wired.com/watch/how-interpreters-do-their-job>.

Orlando, M. 2014, 'A study on the amenability of digital pen technology in a hybrid mode of interpreting: consec-simul with notes', *Translation & Interpreting*, vol. 6, no. 2, pp. 39–54.

Ozolins, U. 2016, 'The myth of the myth of invisibility?', *Interpreting*, vol. 18, no. 2, pp. 273–84. doi:10.1075/intp.18.2.06ozo.

de Pedro Ricoy, R. and Shamy, M. 2017, 'Retrospective protocols: tapping into the minds of interpreting trainees', *Translation and Interpreting*, vol. 9, no. 1, pp. 51–71.

Pielmeyer, H. 2017, 'Interpreting delivery platforms: should you get on the bandwagon?', *ATA interpreters division*, 28 February. <http://www.ata-divisions.org/ID/interpreting-delivery-platforms-get-bandwagon/>.

Plevoets, K. and Defrancq, B. 2016, 'The effect of informational load on disfluencies in interpreting', *Translation and Interpreting Studies. The Journal of the American Translation and Interpreting Studies Association*, vol. 11, no. 2, pp. 202–24.

Pöchhacker, F. and Shlesinger, M. 2002, *The interpreting studies reader*, Routledge.

Pym, A. 2008, 'On omission in simultaneous interpreting. Risk analysis of a hidden effort', in Hansen, G., Chesterman, A., and Gerzymisch-Arbogast, H. (eds.), *Efforts and models in interpreting and translation research: a tribute to Daniel Gile*, John Benjamins, Amsterdam, pp. 83–105.

Pym, A. 2011, 'What technology does to translating', *Translation & Interpreting*, vol. 3, no. 1, pp. 1–9.

Pym, A. 2012, *(1) Spoken and written in conference interpreting, Part 1 – YouTube*, Monterrey Institute of International Studies, USA. <https://www.youtube.com/watch?v=lF8VXzEit2U>.

Reddy, M. J. 1979, 'The conduit metaphor: a case of frame conflict in our language about language', *Metaphor and thought*, vol. 2, pp. 164–201.

Reithofer, K. 2010, 'English as a lingua franca vs. interpreting: battleground or peaceful coexistence?', *The Interpreters' Newsletter*, no. 15, pp. 143–157.

Reithofer, K. 2013, 'Comparing modes of communication: the effect of English as a lingua franca vs. interpreting', *Interpreting*, vol. 15, no. 1, pp. 48–73.

Roy, C. B. 1992, 'A sociolinguistic analysis of the interpreter's role in simultaneous talk in a face-to-face interpreted dialogue', *Sign Language Studies*, vol. 74, pp. 21–61.

Roy, C. B. 1999, *Interpreting as a discourse process*, Oxford University Press, New York.

Seeber, K. 2016, *Review of: conference interpreting: a complete course by R. Setton and A. Dawrant, aiic.net*. <//aiic.net/page/7798>.

Seeber, K. G. 2017, 'Multimodal processing in simultaneous interpreting', in Schweiter, J. W. and Ferreira, A. (eds.), *The handbook of translation and cognition*, John Wiley & sons, Hoboken, NJ, pp. 461–75.

Seeber, K. G. and Kerzel, D. 2011, 'Cognitive load in simultaneous interpreting: model meets data', *International Journal of Bilingualism*, doi:10.1177/1367006911402982.

Seleskovitch, D. 1968, *L'Interprète dans les conférences internationales: problèmes de langage et de communication*, Lettres Modernes.

Seleskovitch, D. 1975, *Langage, langues et mémoire: étude de la prise de notes en interprétation consécutive*, Lettres Modernes.

Seleskovitch, D. 1977, 'Why interpreting is not tantamount to translating languages', *The Incorporated Linguist*, vol. 16, no. 2, pp. 27–33.

Seleskovitch, D. and Lederer, M. 1984, *Interpreter pour traduire*, Pub. de la Sorbonne.

Setton, R. and Dawrant, A. 2016, *Conference interpreting: a complete course*, John Benjamins Publishing Company.

Shannon, C. E. 1948, 'A mathematical theory of communication', *Bell System Technical Journal*, vol. 27, no. 3, pp. 379–423. doi:10.1002/j.1538-7305.1948.tb01338.x.

Siemens, G. 2005, 'Connectivism: a learning theory for the digital age', *International Journal of Instructional Technology and Distance Learning Go Top*, vol. 2, no. 1. <http://itdl.org/Journal/Jan_05/article01.htm>.

Slator. 2018, *Simultaneous interpreters may soon get real-time help just when they need it, Slator*. <https://slator.com/academia/simultaneous-interpreters-may-soon-get-real-time-help-just-when-they-need-it/>.

Sreelekha, S., Bhattacharyya, P. and Malathi, D. 2018, 'Statistical vs. Rule-based machine translation: a comparative study on Indian languages', Subhransu Sekhar Das, Swagatam Das, Panigrahi B. (eds.), *International conference on intelligent computing and applications. Advances in intelligent systems and computing*, vol. 632. Springer, Singapore, pp. 663–75.

Svenstrup, D., Jørgensen, H. L. and Winther, O. 2015, 'Rare disease diagnosis: a review of web search, social media and large-scale data-mining approaches', *Rare Diseases*, vol. 3, no. 1, p. e1083145.

Tate, G. and Turner, G. H. 1997, 'The code and the culture: sign language interpreting-In search of the new breed's ethics', *Deaf worlds*, vol. 13, pp. 27–34.

Taylor, C. 2012, *Google translate turns obama into bush, Mashable*. <https://mashable.com/2012/08/20/google-obama-into-bush/>.

Tiselius, E. 2013, *Experience and expertise in conference interpreting: an investigation of Swedish conference interpreters*, University of Bergen.

Toral, A. et al. 2018, 'Attaining the unattainable? Reassessing claims of human parity in neural machine translation', *arXiv preprint arXiv:1808.10432*.

Torres Díaz, M. G. and Ghignoli, A. 2014, 'Interpreting performed by professionals of other fields: the case of sports commentators', in *The second conference on non-professional interpreting and translation (NPIT2)*, Gemersheim, Germany. <http://dspace.uma.es/xmlui/handle/10630/8130>.

Turner, G. H. 1995, 'The bilingual, bimodal courtroom: a first glance', *Journal of Interpretation*, vol. 7, no. 1, pp. 3–34.

Turner, G. H. 2005, 'Towards real interpreting', in Marschark, M., Peterson, R., and Winston, E. (eds.), *Sign language interpreting and interpreter education: directions for research and practice*, Oxford University Press, New York, pp. 253–65.

Vigouroux, C. B. 2010, 'Double-mouthed discourse: interpreting, framing, and participant roles', *Journal of Sociolinguistics*, vol. 14, no. 3, pp. 341–69.

Wadensjö, C. 1992, *Interpreting as interaction: on dialogue-interpreting in immigration hearings and medical encounters*, Linköping University.

Wadensjö, C. 1998, *Interpreting as interaction*, Longman.

Wilcox, S. and Shaffer, B. 2005, 'Towards a cognitive model of interpreting', in Janzen, T. (ed.), *Topics in signed languages interpreting: theory and practice*, John Benjamins, pp. 27–50.

Zimanyi, K. 2009, 'A diagrammatic approach to redefining the role of the interpreter based on a case study in forensic psychology', *Translation & Interpreting*, vol. 1, no. 2, pp. 55–70.

Zwischenberger, C. 2015, 'Simultaneous conference interpreting and a supernorm that governs it all', *Meta: Journal des traducteurs/Meta:Translators' Journal*, vol. 60, no. 1, pp. 90–111.

Index

For Product Safety Concerns and Information please contact our EU
representative GPSR@taylorandfrancis.com
Taylor & Francis Verlag GmbH, Kaufingerstraße 24, 80331 München, Germany